TORAH

THE FOUNDATIONS OF JUDAISM:

Method, Teleology, Doctrine

PART THREE: *Doctrine*

TORAH

From Scroll to Symbol
in Formative Judaism

JACOB NEUSNER

FORTRESS PRESS   PHILADELPHIA

Quotations from *Pesiqta de R. Kahana* 19:4, trans. W. Braude and Israel J. Kapstein (Philadelphia: Jewish Publication Society of America, 1975), are used by permission of the publisher.

Library of Congress Cataloging in Publication Data

Neusner, Jacob, 1932–
    Torah : from scroll to symbol in formative Judaism.

    (Foundations of Judaism : method, teleology, doctrine ; pt. 3)
    Includes index.
    1. Judaism—History—Talmudic period, 10–425.
    2. Rabbinical literature—History and criticism.
    3. Torah (The Hebrew word) I. Title. II. Series:
Neusner, Jacob, 1932–   . Foundations of Judaism ;
pt. 3
BM601.N48   1983 pt. 3   [BM177]   296 s[296.1]   84–45190
ISBN 0–8006–0734–1

K972F84   Printed in the United States of America   1–734

For
"Patchi"
Avraham Shapira
of
Kibbutz Yizreel
The State of Israel

. . . from the age that is past,
to the age that is waiting before . . .

Contents

Preface

Judaism as we know it at the end of late antiquity reached its now familiar definition when "the Torah" lost its capital letter and definite article and ultimately became "*torah*." What for nearly a millennium had been a particular scroll or book thus came to serve as a symbol of an entire system. When a rabbi spoke of *torah*, he no longer meant only a particular object, a scroll and its contents. Now he used the word to encompass a distinctive and well-defined world view and way of life. Torah now stood for something one does. Knowledge of the Torah promised not merely information about what people were supposed to do, but ultimate redemption or salvation. The shift in the use of the word, accomplished in a particular set of writings out of Judaism in late antiquity, appears dramatically in the following tale drawn from the last document to enter the canon, the Babylonian Talmud:

> R. Kahana [a disciple] went and hid under Rab's [his master's] bed. Hearing Rab "discoursing" and joking with his wife . . . , [Kahana] said to [Rab], "You would think that Abba's [Rab's] mouth had never before tasted the dish." [Rab] said to [Kahana], "Kahana, are you here? Get out! This is disgraceful!" [Kahana] replied, "My lord, it is a matter of *torah*, and I have the need to learn" (b. Ber. 62a).

As soon as we ask ourselves what the word *torah* means in such a context, we recognize the shift captured by the story. For—to state the obvious—to study "the Torah," meaning Scripture, one need not practice cultic voyeurism.

If, however, *torah* came to stand for something other than the particular writings comprising the ancient Israelite Scriptures, how do we trace the shift in content and usage? Clearly, the progress of the word and its meanings, both denotative and connotative, demands our attention. Within the expansion and revision of the word, originally referring to a set of books but in the end encompassing how one is to do even the most intimate deeds, we uncover the formative history of the Judaism for which the word Torah stands. That is the Judaism of the "one whole Torah," both written and oral, of "Moses, our rabbi"—Judaism as it has flourished from late antiquity to our own day.

When we take up the issue at hand, therefore, we confront the symbol that stands for the kind of Judaism presented by the Talmuds and related literature, defined by the authority of the rabbis who stand behind those documents, and best described as "the way of Torah." So far as outsiders supply the name of a religion, the one at hand may be called "rabbinic Judaism," or "talmudic Judaism," for its principal authority figure or authoritative document, or "normative Judaism," for the definitive theological status of the formulation at hand in the life of the Jewish people. But so far as insiders name the religion, that is, find language to capture and encompass the whole of what they do and believe, it is, as Kahana's statement tells us, "torah"—"and I have the need to learn."

The method of this book is conventional and simple. I ask about the meanings various documents impute to a single word. I systematically classify and interpret the answers, so comparing one document to the next. The (more than occasionally) tedious task of consulting concordances for various rabbinical compositions and surveying the use of the word in documents lacking concordances yields facts that demand description and interpretation. The process of determining the meaning of a word in a given context requires little subjective evaluation but sustained objective elimination of impossible meanings. To give an example deriving from a front-page newspaper story, when we are told that "a brilliant filly" has died, we must ask what the adjective "brilliant" contributes to the noun "filly." Since a young mare can hardly have scored exceptionally high grades on an intelligence test, some other meaning must be implied. Along these same lines, we simply ask what a given noun can possibly mean in each distinct context, with the sole proviso that we take nothing for granted. That is, if we did not know what the word Torah would ultimately come to mean, in the full and rich sense imputed to it by the entire corpus of rabbinical writings at the end of their formative history, then what meaning should we uncover only in the particular passage at hand?

What "Torah" can mean, for example, in the mouth of Kahana, as he crawled out from under Rab's bed, is hardly self-evident. And how that word gained the entire burden of abstract meanings associated with it in the fullness of the kind of Judaism at hand is not yet known. The answers to these questions will provide us with the history of the principal doctrine of Judaism as we know it: all canonical writings of rabbis alike form statements of Torah. In the mythic formulation: "When God revealed Torah to Moses at Mount Sinai, God included the most recent and current convictions of authoritative living rabbis." Upon that myth—the Torah-myth—rests the entirety of the system and structure of Judaism in its "classical," "rabbinical," "talmudic," "normative" formulation. The symbol of Torah defines Judaism as we know it. So, since the encompassing doctrine of Judaism is the doctrine of Torah, we shall trace the symbolic development of that doctrine in this final part of my account of the foundations of Judaism.

Since this book forms the third and last in a trilogy, I conclude my prefatory remarks with a picture of how the three books fit together and present a consistent and integrated result. To state in a few words my conception of the history of the formation of Judaism as we know it: I see two distinct stages. First came the question, second the answer.

The question confronted by our sages of blessed memory emerged from Mishnah (ca. 200 C.E.) and the documents most closely associated with it: Abot (ca. 250 C.E.), the Tosefta (ca. 300–50 C.E.), the so-called "tannaitic midrashim" (ca. 300–50 C.E.). (We do not know whether these collections actually derive from the time of the authorities named in them. We only know for sure that those compilations fall within precisely the doctrinal taxa in which the Mishnah, Abot, and Tosefta find their place; in that sense, they may be called "tannaitic," that is, closely associated with the viewpoints of the authorities, Tannas, of the Mishnah itself.) The question that emerges from this aggregate of rabbinical writings focuses upon the Mishnah itself: What is this document? Where does it come from? What is its authority?

The answer to the question then appears in the pages of the two Talmuds, the Talmud of the Land of Israel (ca. 400 C.E.) and the Talmud of Babylonia (ca. 600 C.E.), and in certain collections of scriptural exegesis composed from the formation of the first to that of the second Talmud, ca. 400–600 C.E. The answers provided by this second and distinct aggregate of writings, mainly within the two Talmuds, tell us that the Mishnah is part of the Torah. It comes from Sinai. It enjoys the authority of God's instruction to Moses. In the course of giving those answers, the talmudic (as distinct from the Mishnaic) circle of writings created the doctrine of Judaism as received and believed from the fifth and sixth centuries to the twentieth.

The advent of the Mishnah thus provoked the laying down of the foundations of Judaism as outlined by the sages. The result is in three basic dimensions.

First, the question of status of the Mishnah generated the answer of the creation of distinctive modes of exegesis, and the classification and organization of exegesis, systematically applied first to Mishnah, then to Scripture. That is the result of *Midrash in Context: Exegesis in Formative Judaism.*

Second, the question of the purpose of Israel's life, answered by the Mishnah's framers through an ahistorical teleology that differs from the established eschatology, provoked the Mishnah's heirs and successors to rethink the entire question of teleology. This they did by reframing the inherited eschatology, reshaping in accord with the ontological emphasis of the Mishnah itself the symbol of the Messiah and the mass of diverse doctrines about his coming and his role. Not only was a message of salvation at the end of time grafted onto a doctrine of the centrality of sanctification in an ahistorical ontology of unchanging natural-supernatural eternity in the here and now. The available salvific doctrines were made over so as to serve a system of sanctification. That is the result of *Messiah in Context: Israel's History and Destiny in Formative Judaism.*

And, third, the inherited doctrine of the Torah as a canon of Scripture, attested in Israelite writings of diverse origin in the centuries from the fifth B.C.E. to the second C.E., underwent radical revision. The word Torah ceased to refer in particular to a scroll and its contents. The advent of the Mishnah, demanding entry into the canon, carried with it the need to reframe the meaning of the word Torah. Once the narrow, literary limits of the word had given way, "Torah" came to encompass an entire way of life. The word Torah then served to differentiate not merely one book from another, but one ontic status from another. So Torah not only encompassed a broader range of existence than formerly; it also drew within itself the entire doctrinal heritage of the movement set in motion by the closure of the Mishnah. True, the word Torah continued to denote what it had for so very long. But it also began to connote more things, both concrete and abstract, than anyone had earlier implied. Just as Wisdom in its day served the wisdom tradition of ancient Israel, the word Torah now served to symbolize whatever sages wished to say about the salvation and sanctification of Israel. That is the result of the present book.

With these three results, my theory of the formation of Judaism has found as full expression as I can presently provide: In the beginning was the Mishnah. But in the end, the Talmud, in particular the Talmud of Babylonia, would impart to the Mishnah that full and final meaning—exegetical, teleological, doctrinal—that the Mishnah, as integral component of the one whole Torah of Moses our rabbi, ever was to have.

So the formative history of Judaism yields precisely the result that the traditional history of Judaism has always narrated, with only a few minor modifications.

This brief account of the three volumes of the trilogy may serve for the moment. I hope someday to state in a single, cogent way the main results and conclusions of my somewhat sizable picture of the foundation of Judaism. But these three books will be read one by one, and there is no reason to make each one of them address more than a single question. Having explained what I conceive to be the method of Judaism at its foundations—namely, the method of midrash—and how I imagine that method to have come into being in a literary setting; having provided an account of the teleology of Judaism at its foundations—namely, the doctrine of a messiah reframed within the dimensions of the Torah; I now turn to the principal symbol of the whole. I show, once more, the stages by which it took shape.

The results of the three books, not surprisingly, do correlate with one another. They further point to a single moment, at which Judaism as we know it took shape, and to the requirements of which "our sages of blessed memory" responded. I believe the formative moment lay in the later fourth and earlier fifth centuries. What marked the age was the final triumph of Christianity, joined to the beginning of the redefinition of the political and social setting of the Jews and of Judaism. But to relate the formation of Judaism to the crisis of the nation, Israel, at what turned out to be the dawn of a protracted and difficult history—that is another story, and I cannot tell it here.

JACOB NEUSNER

Acknowledgments

My student, Mrs. Judith Romney Wegner, edited the second draft of the entire manuscript and made many valuable improvements in style.

My dear teacher, colleague, and friend, Jonathan Z. Smith, University of Chicago, kindly read and annotated the manuscript. He is a marvelous critic, and a generous friend. Would that I had the intellect to respond adequately to all of his questions and observations.

My former student and now close co-worker and friend, William Scott Green, read the manuscript and made a number of excellent observations.

Since this is the third and final volume of my trilogy, I am justified in expressing my thanks and admiration to the staff of Fortress Press. I cannot point to an unhappy experience with any editor or publisher in the past quarter-century, but the encounter with Norman Hjelm and his co-workers at Fortress has proved especially fortunate in all ways.

J. N.

Abbreviations

Ah.	Ahilot	Kil.	Kilayim
Am.	Amos	Lam.	Lamentations
Ar.	Arakhin	Lev.	Leviticus
A.Z.	Abodah Zarah	Ma.	Maaserot
B.B.	Baba Batra	Mak.	Makkot
Bekh.	Bekhorot	Mal.	Malachi
Ber.	Berakhot	Me.	Meilah
Bes.	Besah	Meg.	Megillah
Bik.	Bikkurim	Mekh.	Mekhilta
B.M.	Baba Mesia	Men.	Menahot
B.Q.	Baba Qamma	Miq.	Miqvaot
1 Chron.	1 Chronicles	M.Q.	Moed Qatan
Dan.	Daniel	Naz.	Nazir
Dem.	Demai	Ned.	Nedarim
Deut.	Deuteronomy	Neg.	Negaim
Ed.	Eduyyot	Nid.	Niddah
Er.	Erubin	Num.	Numbers
Ex.	Exodus	Or.	Orlah
Ez.	Ezekiel	Par.	Parah
Gen.	Genesis	Pe.	Peah
Git.	Gittin	Pes.	Pesahim
Hab.	Habakkuk	Prov.	Proverbs
Hag.	Hagigah	Ps.	Psalms
Hal.	Hallah	Qid.	Qiddushin
Hor.	Horayot	Qin.	Qinnim
Hos.	Hosea	Qoh.	Qohelet
Hul.	Hullin	R.H.	Rosh Hashanah
Is.	Isaiah	1 Sam.	1 Samuel
Jer.	Jeremiah	San.	Sanhedrin
Kel. B.Q.	Kelim	Shab.	Shabbat
Ker.	Kerithot	Sheb.	Shebiit
Ket.	Ketubot	Shebu.	Shebuot

Sheq.	Sheqalim	Toh.	Tohorot
Sot.	Sotah	T.Y.	Tebul Yom
Suk.	Sukkah	Y.	Yerushalmi
Ta.	Taanit	Yad.	Yadim
Tam.	Tamid	Yeb.	Yebamot
Tem.	Temurah	Zab.	Zabim
Ter.	Terumot	Zeb.	Zebahim

Note on Bibliography

The bibliographical apparatus serving a study of the word "Torah" as well as the concept it represents is enormous. The number of books and articles on the meaning of the word "Torah" in a *given* rabbinic document, the Mishnah, the Talmud of the Land of Israel, the Tosefta, and the like, is not. Indeed, I cannot point to a single book or article in any language that asks the question addressed in the substantive chapters of this book. Earlier books of mine include many pages of bibliography, relevant, in a general way, to this one. A simple topic, such as "Judaism," after all, would demand attention to a not-inconsiderable corpus of scholarly writing, much of it of high quality. Yet if I list only the books I found useful in working on this book in particular—and this is what a bibliography should list—I have to include only concordances, all of them cited *ad loc.*, editions of texts, translations, and the like. When we get past the apparatus of scholarly inquiry serving any topic in the study of the formative centuries of Judaism, for the issue of this book, for the problem at hand, I know of not a single relevant book or article. That is why this book contains no bibliography, only an apology for the absence of one.

TORAH

INTRODUCTION:

From Scroll to Symbol

A well-composed religious system will express in all of its details the main points of insistence of the whole. The sort of holy building people build, the sort of holy activity they deem worthwhile, the sort of consecrated family life they propagate, the sort of holy leader they envisage, the sort of holy community they form, and the sort of life beyond this life they promise—all express an essentially harmonious and cogent conviction. To state matters simply, everything repeats everything. Myth explains ritual. Ritual expresses myth. The histories of Judaisms—various religious systems, related to the same Scripture, produced by the people Israel, and intended to organize and make sense in supernatural categories of the historical life of that people—yield more than a few apt examples of well-composed religious systems.

One striking example derives from the Judaism of our own day. If we walk into any synagogue anywhere, our eye focuses upon what is in every synagogue the visual center: an ark containing a scroll, a Torah-scroll, a scroll containing the five books attributed to Moses. If we then ask what sort of activity the synagogue fosters, under all circumstances people speak of praying and studying the Torah, both activities falling within the same classification. If we inquire into who provides the leadership and how such a person qualifies, it is a rabbi, defined as one (usually male) who has mastered and now teaches the Torah. True, synagogue life consists of much more than classes of students who study the Torah. But the principal, and integrating, point of insistence stresses the act of studying a particular document in a particular way and doing what the rabbi says it ordains. Accordingly, Judaism as we know it presents itself to the world as the way of the Torah: studying the Torah and doing what the Torah commands.

Now when we turn back in time and ask about the origins of this Torah-centered form of Judaism, we move rapidly through the centu-

1

ries from the twentieth through the nineteenth, eighteenth, and so on. All evidence from all places in which the people Israel has flourished yields essentially the same picture of Judaism. It was a religious system in which rabbis taught the Torah and governed the community in accordance with its theology and law. And yet, when we take account of what we know about the people Israel in ancient times, from its beginnings down to late antiquity, we realize that matters then were hardly as they have been for so many later centuries. When, for instance, we take up the sources of Judaism in the Near East in the ninth and tenth centuries, we find that "Torah" does not then stand for all the things it represents for most Jews later on. Controversy centered upon the canonicity of part of the Torah—the oral part, not written in the Pentateuch but gathered in the Talmuds and related literature. Accordingly, in our movement back through time, as we approach late antiquity, the world before Islam, we encounter the last stirrings of the struggle over the doctrine, hence also over the principal symbol, of Judaism that had earlier raged.

Moving rapidly over the formative centuries of Judaism as we know it, that is, the first seven centuries C.E., we reach a period before the age in which the Torah formed the principal symbol and visual center alike for a community of Jews. Indeed, we can identify a number of groups for which the Torah, while accepted as God's revelation to Moses at Sinai, competed with other modes of symbolization and other mythic messages entirely. Thus, were the Essenes whose library survived at Qumran to tell us what kind of building they would build for themselves, it surely would not take the form of a synagogue in town or village. We know that it took the form of a communal structure in the wilderness. In that building they studied Torah, to be sure. But their teacher was expected to do things rabbis rarely have been supposed to do. The life of the community followed paths that later Jews hardly explored. Again, during that phase of Christian history, in which Christianity formed a sector of the life of Israel, that group of Jews, while also revering the Torah as a mode of consecration, met around a table and ate cultic meals. To be sure, people taught the Torah. But the visual center, the expressive symbol, did not consist of a scroll; learning proved ancillary to other, more important acts, such as celibacy and martyrdom like that of Christ. A simple mental experiment, in which we asked diverse sorts of Jews in antiquity to tell us in a few words what they stood for, would yield a far broader range of symbolic systems than the Torah-centered one that has prevailed for so long. The result of that experiment defines the problem at hand. Let me spell it out.

The Torah of Moses clearly occupied a critical place in all systems of Judaism from the closure of the Torah-book, the Pentateuch, in the time of Ezra onward. But in late antiquity, for one group alone the book developed into an abstract and encompassing symbol, so that in the Judaism that took shape in the formative age, the first seven centuries C.E., everything was contained in that one thing. How so? When we speak of *torah*, in rabbinical literature of late antiquity, we no longer denote a particular book, on the one side, or the contents of such a book, on the other. Instead, we connote a broad range of clearly distinct categories of noun and verb, concrete fact and abstract relationship alike. "Torah" stands for a kind of human being. It connotes a social status and a sort of social group. It refers to a type of social relationship. It further denotes a legal status and differentiates among legal norms. As symbolic abstraction, the word encompasses things and persons, actions and status, points of social differentiation and legal and normative standing, as well as "revealed truth." In all, the main points of insistence of the whole of Israel's life and history come to full symbolic expression in that single word. If people wanted to explain how they would be saved, they would use the word Torah. If they wished to sort out their parlous relationships with gentiles, they would use the word Torah. Torah stood for salvation and accounted for Israel's this-worldly condition and the hope, for both individual and nation alike, of life in the world to come. For the kind of Judaism under discussion, therefore, the word Torah stood for everything. The Torah symbolized the whole, at once and entire. When, therefore, we wish to describe the unfolding of the definitive doctrine of Judaism in its formative period, the first exercise consists in paying close attention to the meanings imputed to a single word.

To summarize the argument up to this point: The way of life and world view propagated by the Judaism represented by the principal documents of the formative age, the late second century through the seventh, stand alone in their focus upon the Torah. Other Judaisms, in which the Torah had its place as an element of divine service, built synagogues. The framers of the sort of Judaism at hand, called "rabbinic," from the honorific accorded its principal heroes, or "talmudic," from the title of its main literary record, or "classical" and "normative," by reference to the theological evaluation later accorded to it, built master-disciple Torah study circles. Others merely revered the Torah. The religious movement at hand took over the Torah and rewrote it in far broader terms than anyone else had ever imagined. Many kinds of Judaism believed in life after death and a world to come. But this distinctive sort of Judaism taught that, after death and in heaven, the Jews would study Torah under the direction of Moses and God. For ordinary Israelites, the biological father was the natural father and God in heaven the supernatural one. For this special sector of Israel, the master—the teacher, the rabbi—served as a supernatural father, taking priority over the this-worldly, natural one.

So, as is clear, every detail of the religious system at hand exhibits essentially the same point of insistence, captured in the simple notion of the Torah as the generative symbol, the total, exhaustive expression of the system as a whole. That is why the definitive ritual consisted in studying the Torah through the rites of discipleship. The definitive myth explained that one who studied Torah would become holy, like Moses "our rabbi," and like God, in whose image humanity was made and whose Torah provided the plan and the model for what God wanted of a humanity created in his image. As Christians saw in Christ God made flesh, so the framers of the system of Judaism at hand found in the Torah that image of God to which Israel should aspire, and to which the sage in fact conformed.

In describing matters thus, I present a composite picture of how things were to emerge at the end of the formative age of the kind of Judaism under discussion. But we cannot take for granted that the way things came out at the end is how they always were. On the contrary, as soon as we recognize the novelty of the symbolic system of a Judaism expressed through new uses of the word Torah, the cultic activity of Torah-study, and the supernatural relationship of disciple to master of the Torah, we ask how it took shape. The system at hand, while absorbing much from its predecessors, was hardly congruent with anything that had gone before. Like earlier systems in some ways, unlike them in others, the talmudic-rabbinic-classical Judaism used the old in new ways and presented the whole fresh, an unprecedented system and structure.

Let me now spell out the particular modest contribution I hope to make in this book. It is to differentiate, among the documents that constitute the canon of Judaism in its formative era, the uses and

meanings of the word Torah. The reader and I will work systematically through the ways in which the word is used. We do so in order
to locate the points, within the unfolding canon, at which potentiali-
ties of the symbol of Torah are realized stage by stage. When we find
the word Torah speaking of a world beyond a scroll, so that it constitutes not an object and its contents, but an abstract category or classification, Judaism as we know it will have come to full expression.
When Torah stands for a way of life, a kind of human status, a sort of
relationship, holiness embodied in persons and encountered in the
streets and kitchens and bedrooms (to speak anachronistically), then
Torah will have transcended its original meaning and limitation. Torah at that point ceases to denote a scroll and to connote revelation. It
has begun to denote a symbol, the abstraction of relationship and classification of "way of life." Torah then connotes the whole normative
doctrine, the value system, we today call "Judaism." To state the argument simply: *when Torah becomes taxon, Judaism is born.* So we
go in search of how a word changes its meanings in a sequence of documents. But what we seek to know is not philology, it is rather how
the historical formation of a religious tradition emerges from meanings imputed to a word.

The work at hand required the survey and classification of the usages of the word Torah as revealed in concordances. The labor proved
tedious. I fear that reports of the results may not turn out much more
interesting. Yet I know no other way to make my point. When I assert
that the word Torah exhibits one limited set of meanings in a given
document, I have to show how all usages of the word fall into the taxa
I claim as exhaustive classifications. Documents to which we do not
yet enjoy access through concordances naturally produce less decisive
evidence, particularly the Talmud of the Land of Israel. Here I have
given a few examples of the use of the word, rather than pretend,
through the inevitably faulty impressions of the naked eye, to give a
complete list. So where we do not have concordances, results are necessarily impressionistic. Nonetheless, I have given an ample selection
of illustrations of how the word Torah appears.

So, in all, the book unfolds as a kind of protracted research report,
with some further reflections and observations based upon the results. I ask a simple question. I give as full and responsible an answer
as I can. This is the best way I know to describe the history of the doctrine of Judaism in its formative centuries, in the context of the com-

plementary components of its method and teleology. These three components together constitute the foundation—that is, the basis—for the Judaism that took shape in late antiquity and remained definitive thereafter. I offer a picture of beginnings that I hope will, in time, generate a much more sophisticated theory of Judaism.

The sequence of documents is easy to explain. It is not my own invention. The Mishnah is the first document of the Judaism under study. For its part, the Mishnah refers back only to "Sinai," so to speak, that is, to the Pentateuch and some later biblical writings. It makes ample use of facts invented from the formation of the Pentateuch to its own day but acknowledges the source (outside of Scripture) of none of them. So we begin where the system at hand begins.

We proceed to the documents that stand in the rabbinic canon closest to the Mishnah. First comes Abot, a compilation of Torah-sayings associated with the Mishnah and generally understood to constitute its first apologetic. Since the latest named authorities of Abot derive from the period a generation or two after Judah the Patriarch, "Our holy Rabbi" or simply "Rabbi," who flourished at about 200 C.E., we may date Abot at about 250 C.E. In the same category as Abot, namely, serving essentially as an internal amplification and paraphrastic exegesis of the Mishnah, the Tosefta, meaning supplements (that is, additions to the Mishnah), derives from a later period. All of its named authorities are regarded as stemming from the same age as the Mishnah. Hence they enjoy the same status of authority. But, since the document cites the Mishnah verbatim, its time of closure must be post-Mishnaic. While we do not know exactly when the Tosefta reached its final form, if we assume the fourth century, we shall not err by much. In that same setting we should locate, also, Abot de R. Nathan, the Fathers according to Rabbi Nathan, an amplification of Abot.

Generally thought to have come to redaction at about 400, the Talmud of the Land of Israel (a/k/a "the Palestinian Talmud," "the Yerushalmi") forms the first great exegetical work, devoted to the Mishnah, to take up an independent stance vis-à-vis the Mishnah. That is to say, while the Tosefta paraphrases sentences of the Mishnah in its own way, the Talmud of the Land of Israel will cite those sentences of Mishnah, as well as of the Tosefta, and then introduce its own mode of discourse to provide an exegesis of a closed canon: Mishnah-Tosefta. So the framers of the Tosefta claim to speak within, or at least alongside, the Mishnah, while the authors of the Talmud of the Land of Israel treat antiphonally both Mishnah and Tosefta: them, *then us*, then them, *then us*. The Talmud of the Land of Israel thus cites the Mishnah and the Tosefta (though less thoroughly) phrase by phrase and line by line, and so it treats the Mishnah and the Tosefta as closed books. In this respect, the first of the two Talmuds differs from the Tosefta, which insinuates its ideas into the Mishnah by rephrasing or internally glossing the Mishnah's sentences. It also differs from Abot, which, when speaking of "Torah," may mean (at least among other things) the Mishnah as a whole. The Talmud of the Land of Israel for its part never treats the Mishnah as a complete document. Rather, its framers dissect the Mishnah into its smallest component parts.

The Talmud of the Land of Israel, in point of fact, presents two different approaches to the Mishnah. One, as I just explained, is to organize discourse around episodic, line-by-line exegesis of the text. The other is to construct thematic essays on jurisprudential problems generated by philosophizing about general principles of law, solved by reference to specific passages of the Mishnah. This mode of exegesis treats the materials of the Mishnah as incidental to the issue at hand.

The rabbinic canon includes more than the Mishnah and systematic exegesis of its contents in the associated literature just surveyed. There is a second focus of discourse, another source of doctrine. That—not surprisingly—is Scripture, "the written Torah" in the language of later rabbinic myth. At about the time—ca. 400 C.E.—that the Talmud of the Land of Israel undertook systematic exegesis of the Mishnah, organizing matters around a line-by-line exposition of passages of Mishnah read in sequence, a parallel enterprise proceeded to do for Scripture precisely what was done for the Mishnah. With special reference first of all to the Pentateuch, the work commonly called midrash produced units of discourse of just those types paramount in the exegesis of the Mishnah: (1) line-by-line exegesis, on the one side, and (2) abstract thematic discourse about themes or theological principles, referring to a wide range of passages, on the other.

We are not entirely sure about the order in which the various collections of pentateuchal and other scriptural exegesis took shape. They fall, however, into taxa defined by the paramount traits of discourse characteristic of the several documents. Still, as I have suggested, if we were to guess that the compositions of exegesis of

Scripture were worked out from the time the Talmud of the Land of Israel was written and over the next two hundred years, that is, from ca. 400 to 600 C.E., I believe we should not err by much. Accordingly, our next categories are compositions of exegesis of Scripture, parallel to the above-named compositions of exegesis of Mishnah, the Tosefta, and the Talmud of the Land of Israel, and worked out along essentially the same redactional lines.

These collections of scriptural exegesis fall into three categories, differentiated, as I explained, by formal-exegetical logoi—from concrete, verbatim explanation of words and phrases to abstract speculative ratiocination about topics or themes. The first category consists of exegesis in which the exegete takes a passage of Scripture and explains its sentences, line by line, sometimes citing, sometimes amplifying. The second category consists of rather wide-ranging abstract discourses upon themes of Scripture, in which the exegete weaves filigrees of verses of Scripture to make points about large-scale theological issues. The third category falls in between, containing both line-by-line exegesis and thematic constructions of discourse.

In chapter 5 I have kept the three groups apart, treating the essentially exegetical compositions by themselves, then the collections combining exegetical and discursive units of discourse, and, finally, the collections of essays of an essentially nonexegetical character. If we could demonstrate that first came the exegetical, then the discursive compositions, the given order would prove chronological and not merely typological. I think it probable that the discursive writings come last. But that speculation remains unproved.

The Talmud of Babylonia marks the conclusion of the formation of the rabbinic canon in late antiquity. It is conventionally dated at about 500 C.E., though no evidence external to the document itself requires our placing a date on the document much before the ninth century C.E. By then, we find clear knowledge of the existence of the Babylonian Talmud, exhibited in writings wholly outside the framework of the Talmud itself. Sticking to established convention, however, we place the Talmud of Babylonia somewhere between 500 and 650 C.E.

The contents of the Talmud of Babylonia assuredly place the document at the end of the formative age. How so? Pretty much anything presented in the other documents we find in this one too. But what we find here we do not necessarily locate elsewhere, in compositions assumed to be of earlier date. The Talmud of Babylonia thus serves as a kind of *summa* and encyclopedia of Torah—that is, of Judaism. It contains almost everything we can demonstrate circulated earlier, while also preserving much else. The Talmud's modes of discourse are four: (1) exegesis of Mishnah and Tosefta, (2) abstract discourse on law in general, (3) exegesis of Scripture and (4) abstract discourse on mythic or theological themes of Scripture in general. So the Talmud of Babylonia joins together the available types of discourse on the Mishnah and on Scripture, making them into a single composition.

In all, therefore, I have made my way through the entire canon of Judaism in its formative age. Once the Talmud of Babylonia reached a conclusion, Judaism—Torah—as we know it had taken shape. True, once formed, the Judaism of Torah would grow and develop. But its fundamental character, its definitive symbolic structure of both myth and law, had reached full development at the time of the closure of the second Talmud. Its laws would grow and change. Its theological and mythic components would flourish in new and unprecedented ways. But its fundamental symbolic structure would endure to our own day, ever changing and always vital, never intact but essentially unimpaired. When, therefore, we know how the principal symbol for the doctrine of Judaism, along with its method and teleology, had reached its full development, we may claim to have outlined, for the first time, if in only a primitive way and through a rough mapping, the foundations of Judaism.

In speaking of foundations, of course, we cannot ignore all that went before. Whether or not the framers of the Mishnah and their successors and continuators admitted it, they certainly were not the first Jews, nor did they speak to the original Israel. On the contrary, the words they used had a long and complex history. At the outset, the framers had to assimilate that history and accommodate themselves to its possibilities. The language they used they did not invent. We therefore offer a very brief account of the way matters stood in the centuries before the great masters of the Mishnah undertook their labor.

Let us rapidly survey "Torah" in its established meanings in ancient Israelite Scripture ("the Old Testament," "Tanakh," or "Written Torah"). Our survey derives from Michael Fishbane's definitive article, "Torah" (*Biblical Encyclopaedia* 8:469–83, in Hebrew). In the pentateuchal stratum, the word Torah serves as a common noun, meaning instruction. In the priestly layer, the word denotes a particular chapter of cultic instructions given to priests—once again, a common noun. In Deuteronomy, by contrast, the word gains a definite article, *the* Torah. But "the Torah" still refers to the stories, speeches, laws, blessings and curses under discussion, as the case may be. Fishbane emphasizes that in the Deuteronomic literature, the word gains an elevated sense. "Torah" encompasses "the incomparable wisdom and understanding of Israel." The other pentateuchal books exhibit no parallel to this usage. The earlier phases of prophecy in writing exhibit the familiar sense of Torah as instruction to priests. An expansion of this meaning occurs in Isaiah, to whom the word means also prophetic instruction or oracle, revelation in a concrete sense, namely, what God has said to the prophet as much as to the priest. In the historical books, Joshua, Judges, Samuel, and Kings, influenced as they are by the Deuteronomic school, the familiar meaning of Torah predominates. The Chroniclers' rewriting of the historical books emphasizes the priestly sense of Torah as instruction for the cult. In the wisdom literature the word Torah meant instruction in practical wisdom. Summarizing the same matter, Louis I. Rabinowitz (*Encyclopaedia Judaica* 15:1235–36) states, "The word is used in different ways but the underlying idea of 'teaching' is common to all."

"Torah" further denotes the Pentateuch as distinct from the rest of the Hebrew Bible, and, later on, in postbiblical writings, refers to the entire Hebrew Scriptures as distinct from writing of lesser standing. James Sanders (*Torah and Canon* [Philadelphia: Fortress Press, 1972], pp. 2ff.) surveys the use of the word Torah in reference to the Pentateuch. The first such clearcut usage, he says, appears in the prologue to Ben Sira, though Ezra and Nehemiah *may* mean the Pentateuch when they use the word Torah. The New Testament writers use the word *nomos*, Law, in both the narrow sense of Pentateuch and the larger sense of "holy scriptures generally." Sanders further finds four different senses of the word Law (*nomos*) in Paul: "(1) in its Greek philosophic sense, (2) in its legalistic sense, (3) in its broader revelatory sense, and (4) as the word symbolizing mainstream Judaism of his time." The word generally refers to authoritative tradition.

As I have stressed, the first document of rabbinic Judaism, the Mishnah, refers backward to Scripture alone, ignoring the intervening centuries of Israelite religious writing from end of the second cen-

tury C.E. backward to the completion of the Torah-book, the Pentateuch, perhaps in the time of Ezra, ca. 450 B.C.E. But while those
nearly seven hundred years (to them fourteen hundred years, going
back to Sinai) proved barren so far as the authors of the Mishnah were
concerned, we may briefly glance at how the word Torah was used by
at least one group in the interval.

Clearly, when the diverse collection of writings began to appear as
a single, closed, and holy Scripture, the usage of the word Torah decisively shifted. The word, for the Essenes at Qumran, as for all others,
came to refer to the Holy Scripture as God's revelation to Israel. The
analogy, within the writings themselves, to the new usage of the word
Torah derives from the Deuteronomic tradition, found both in Deuteronomy and in Joshua, where, as Fishbane points out, Torah bears
the sense of a revealed piece of writing.

The use of Torah to refer to Scripture, or more broadly to what God
has revealed in general, occurs in the Essene hymn No. 7 (column 4
line 10, Vermes, *Dead Sea Scrolls in English*, p. 161; see also Svend
Holm-Nielsen, *Hodayot. Psalms from Qumran* [Aarhus, 1960], pp.
76ff.)

> And they, teachers of lies and seers of falsehood have schemed against
> me a devilish scheme
> to exchange the Torah engraved on my heart by Thee for the smooth
> things (which they speak) to Thy people.
> And they withhold from the thirsty the drink of Knowledge, and as-
> suage their thirst with vinegar. . . .

M. Delcor (*Les hymnes de Qumran* [*Hodayot*] [Paris, 1962]), pp.
140–41) comments that the word Torah refers to the Mosaic law. The
enemies, he says, have attempted not only to turn the people away
from the doctrine of the righteous teacher, but also to alter the Torah,
which they have received from God. The word Torah also occurs
thirteen times in the *Manual of Discipline*, and thirty times in the
Damascus Covenant. Those who join the community, for example,
undertake to keep all the commandments of the Torah of Moses
(Vermes, *Dead Sea Scrolls*, p. 79). In the Damascus Rule, "the well
which the princes dug" (Num. 21:18) is "the Torah," those who dug it
were the converts of Israel; "the stave" of the same passage is the in-
terpreter of the Torah, and so on. When, therefore, we reach the

writings at hand, we find ourselves in familiar territory with "The Torah" as a completed book or scroll, divine revelation subject to systematic interpretation. Matthew Black (*The Scrolls and Christian Origins* [N.Y., 1961; repr. Scholars Press for Brown Judaic Studies, 1983], pp. 120ff., 128ff.) points out that the Essene community at Qumran was known as a "Torah community." The grounds for its secession lay in an attempt to reform the Torah. The Torah was conceived as a completed document, available now for interpretation and application (Black, *Scrolls*, pp. 120–21). Once Torah, that is, Scripture, had reached closure, then the process of exegesis would begin.

This very brief account yields one important fact. Once the ancient Israelite writings had been sorted out, with some of them entering the status of divine instruction and called "Torah," then, but only then, the two now familiar complementary meanings of the word Torah came into being. Torah denoted a particular scroll or set of scrolls, to us a book, and the contents of such a scroll, believed to convey God's will revealed to Israel. At that point, the word Torah referred to a particular object, a scroll. The word then began its long history of expansion and amplification. So, as Fishbane's survey makes clear, before the development of a literature deemed authoritative, that is, a canon, and the identification of that literature with the word Torah, one would have to spell the word Torah with a small T. It would refer to a type, a category, a taxon or set of taxa, a genus and its species. Only when Torah came to denote a particular set of writings and to exclude other writings did the word come to mean the things it meant for the centuries from Ezra to the Mishnah, from ca. 450 B.C.E. to ca. 200 C.E.: a scroll and its contents.

As we shall now see, once the Mishnah came on the scene, people who believed the Mishnah to constitute authoritative law and doctrine had to figure out the relationship of that document to the sole authoritative document they had previously recognized, the Torah, the written Torah revealed by God to Moses at Mount Sinai. Once that question confronted the Mishnah's proponents and authorities, they would answer it by a process of expansion and abstraction. The word Torah (so to speak) lost its capital T, ceasing to refer only to a single thing, a book with its contents. It then came to denote a status and to connote a way of life.

Before proceeding to the body of the study, the reader will want the answers to two questions. First, since I systematically review the usages of the word Torah through the rabbinic corpus, the scope of my review should be explained. Where we have concordances, I survey all, and catalogue most, of the appearances of the word Torah and its synonyms and associated usages, e.g., *oraita*, on the one side, "words of Torah" and the sizable number of other phrases in which the word Torah is used, on the other. Where there are no concordances, as I said—the Yerushalmi is the principal document—I surveyed the usages as best I could. But the scope of the review is significantly limited.

Second, the classifications which I use to explain how the word appears require a word of clarification, even though, as they become important, I spell out their meanings once again. What I did was find in the sequence of documents comprehensive categories for the usage of the word Torah. Then, on the second go-around, I systematically tested those categories that appeared later against the data of the earlier documents. The word Torah refers in the Mishnah to some but not all things, e.g., a particular object, revelation, a particular act, an indicator of status. The word does not refer to two Torahs, one written, the other memorized or oral. It does not bear the connotation of providing salvation. Later on, I found these other usages and introduced them at the outset. In all, I should claim that the classifications at hand emerged solely from the data I examined and rest wholly upon inductive inquiry.

The meaning of the several categories should require only brief explanation.

When the Torah refers to a particular thing, it is to a scroll containing divinely revealed words.

The Torah may further refer to revelation, not as an object but as a corpus of doctrine.

When one "does Torah," the disciple "studies" or "learns," and the master "teaches," Torah. Hence while the word Torah never appears as a verb, it does refer to an act.

The word also bears a quite separate sense, torah as category or classification or corpus of rules, e.g., "the torah of driving a car" is a usage entirely acceptable to some documents. This generic usage of the word does occur. To avoid still more distinct lists than I already give, I have grouped the two senses, Torah as a particular act and Torah as generic, in the same rubric. But they bear no relationship to one another.

The word Torah very commonly refers to a status, distinct from and above another status, as "teachings of Torah" as against "teachings of scribes." For the two Talmuds that distinction is absolutely critical to the entire hermeneutic enterprise. But it is important even in the Mishnah.

Obviously, no account of the meaning of the word Torah can ignore the distinction between the two Torahs, written and oral. Hence I treat that as a distinct classification, even though it is important only in the secondary stages of the formation of the literature.

Finally, the word Torah refers to a source of salvation, often fully worked out in stories about how the individual and the nation will be saved through Torah. In general, the sense of the word "salvation" is not complicated. It is simply salvation in the way in which Deuteronomy and the Deuteronomic historians understand it: kings who do what God wants win battles, those who do not, lose. So too here, people who study and do Torah are saved from sickness and death, and the way Israel can save itself from its condition of degradation also is through Torah.

After my survey of the ways in which the word appears in a given document, I offer some generalizations about the theory of the Torah in that document. Chapter 5 presents three such brief summaries and generalizations, divided among the three types of collections of scriptural exegesis laid out in that chapter.

To me the procedures of the book are simple and self-evidently valid, the results rather pedestrian and expected. But they are not commonplace, and indeed run contrary to what every account of the meaning of the word Torah, and the unfolding and development of that meaning, tells us. The available pictures accurately report how matters came out at the end of the formation of Judaism. But they do not take account of the diversity of opinions and meanings assigned to the word, and symbol, of the Torah, in the several documents that took shape along the way from the Mishnah to the Babylonian Talmud nearly half a millennium later.

It remains only to account for a fact that puzzles me as much as it must surprise the reader. I simply did not know how to provide a bibliography for this book. The reason is that I cannot point to a single article on the meaning of the word Torah as revealed in a given document of the rabbinic corpus in late antiquity. Everyone of course refers to the centrality of "Torah," meaning various things. But the research represented by this book is not into a generalization that "Torah" is an important word, concept, or category in rabbinic Judaism in general. What I wanted to know is what categories encompass the diverse usages, and how each document reveals its relationship to those encompassing categories. Does a given composition use the word in only a few of the ways in which, over all, the word appears? Or does it use the word in all of them? If so, does it use the word in a given category in pretty much the same way that other documents do? Or does it reveal a distinctive usage? As I said, from the issue of the use of the word in the Mishnah in particular to that of the use of the word Torah in the Babylonian Talmud examined by itself, a document written over four hundred years later, I know of not a single book or article in any language. To list all of the items that find their way onto the conventional canon of books on rabbinic Judaism seems to me a waste of time, since I have given ample bibliographies in all of my former books on the same general theme. But then, as I said above, I do not know what else to list. The texts, translations, and, above all, concordances are specified where used. Since here begins the work of differentiation and reconstruction of meanings imputed to the central word and symbol of Judaism, the reader will understand the absence of a bibliography of relevant writings. As I said, I know of no articles or monographs on the use and sense of words in a given document of the rabbinic corpus. Everything done to date synthesizes all sayings and stories from all compositions, early, late, and medieval. When writing about a totality, a "Judaism," then the requirements of discourse about a system and a whole, an -ism, will be met by harmonization.

If, on the other hand, we propose to ask about the sequence in which a given composite took shape—the formation of the -ism—then we have no choice but to dissect and deconstruct. The foundation, then, of reconstruction will emerge on its own. When we see (as best we can) in what context and under what circumstances a given idea or component of an idea first came to expression in our sources, we may then pursue our larger program. We ask whether and how a given idea related or responded to the circumstance in which it made its appearance. We further want to know what lent that same idea continuing credence and made it compelling long after the original setting faded into time. These two questions—original setting, persistence—encompass the whole of the task of describing the formation and ongoing history of the religion at hand. My work then is to describe, analyze, and ultimately, interpret the formation of Judaism: its beginnings, persistence, relevance to the life of Israel, the Jewish people, in times past. I can think of no more correct point of entry than the central and definitive symbol of the whole: the Torah.

1

The Mishnah
and the Torah

FROM CONCRETE TO ABSTRACT

Upon its closure, the Mishnah gained an exalted political status as the constitution of Jewish government of the Land of Israel. Accordingly, the clerks who knew and applied its law had to explain the standing of that law, meaning its relationship to the law of the Torah. But the Mishnah provided no account of itself. Unlike biblical law codes, the Mishnah begins with no myth of its own origin. It ends with no doxology. Discourse commences in the middle of things and ends abruptly. What follows from such laconic mumbling is that the exact status of the document required definition entirely outside the framework of the document itself. The framers of the Mishnah gave no hint of the nature of their book, so the Mishnah reached the political world of Israel without a trace of self-conscious explanation or any theory of validation.

The one thing that is clear, alas, is negative. The framers of the Mishnah nowhere claim, implicitly or explicitly, that what they have written forms part of the Torah, enjoys the status of God's revelation to Moses at Sinai, or even systematically carries forward secondary exposition and application of what Moses wrote down in the wilderness. Later on, I think two hundred years beyond the closure of the Mishnah, the need to explain the standing and origin of the Mishnah led some to posit two things. First, God's revelation of the Torah at Sinai encompassed the Mishnah as much as Scripture. Second, the Mishnah was handed on through oral formulation and oral transmission from Sinai to the framers of the document as we have it. These two convictions, fully exposed in the ninth-century letter of Sherira, in fact emerge from the references of both Talmuds to the dual Torah. One part is in writing. The other was oral and now is in the Mishnah.

As for the Mishnah itself, however, it contains not a hint that any-

17

one has heard any such tale. As we shall see, the earliest apologists for the Mishnah, represented in Abot and the Tosefta alike, know nothing of the fully realized myth of the dual Torah of Sinai. It may be that the authors of those documents stood too close to the Mishnah to see the Mishnah's standing as a problem or to recognize the task of accounting for its origins. Certainly they never refer to the Mishnah as something out there, nor speak of the document as autonomous and complete. Only the two Talmuds reveal that conception—alongside their mythic explanation of where the document came from and why it should be obeyed. In any event, the absence of explicit expression of such a claim in behalf of the Mishnah requires little specification. It is just not there.

But the absence of an implicit claim demands explanation. When ancient Jews wanted to gain for their writings the status of revelation, of *torah*, or at least to link what they thought to what the Torah had said, they could do one of four things. They could sign the name of a holy man of old, for instance, Adam, Enoch, Ezra. They could imitate the Hebrew style of Scripture. They could claim that God had spoken to them. They could, at the very least, cite a verse of Scripture and impute to the cited passage their own opinion. These four methods —pseudepigraphy, stylistic imitation (hence, forgery), claim of direct revelation from God, and eisegesis—found no favor with the Mishnah's framers. To the contrary, they signed no name to their book. Their Hebrew was new in its syntax and morphology, completely unlike that of the Mosaic writings of the Pentateuch. They never claimed that God had anything to do with their opinions. They rarely cited a verse of Scripture as authority. It follows that, whatever the authors of the Mishnah said about their document, the implicit character of the book tells us that they did not claim God had dictated or even approved what they had to say. Why not? The framers simply ignored all the validating conventions of the world in which they lived. And, as I said, they failed to make explicit use of any others.

It follows that we do not know whether the Mishnah was supposed to be part of the Torah or to enjoy a clearly defined relationship to the existing Torah. We also do not know what else, if not the Torah, was meant to endow the Mishnah's laws with heavenly sanction. To state matters simply, we do not know what the framers of the Mishnah said they had made, nor do we know what the people who received and were supposed to obey the Mishnah thought they possessed.

A survey of the uses of the word Torah in the Mishnah, to be sure, provides us with an account of what the framers of the Mishnah, founders of what would emerge as rabbinic Judaism, understood by that term. But it will not tell us how they related their own ideas to the Torah, nor shall we find a trace of evidence of that fully articulated way of life—the use of the word Torah to categorize and classify persons, places, things, relationships, all manner of abstractions —that we find fully exposed in some later redacted writings.

True, the Mishnah places a high value upon studying the Torah and upon the status of the sage. A "*mamzer*-disciple of a sage takes priority over a high-priest *am-haares*," as at M. Hor. 3:8. But that judgment, distinctive though it is, cannot settle the question. All it shows is that the Mishnah pays due honor to the sage. But if the Mishnah does not claim to constitute part of the Torah, then what makes a sage a sage is not mastery of the Mishnah *in particular*. What we have in hand merely continues the established and familiar position of the wisdom writers of old. Wisdom is important. Knowledge of the Torah is definitive. But to maintain that position, one need hardly profess the fully articulated Torah-myth of rabbinic Judaism. Proof of that fact, after all, is the character of the entire wisdom literature prior to the Mishnah itself.

So the issue is clearly drawn. It is not whether we find in the Mishnah exaggerated claims about the priority of the disciple of a sage. We do find such claims. The issue is whether we find in the Mishnah the assertion that whatever the sage has on the authority of his master goes back to Sinai. We seek a definitive view that what the sage says falls into the classification of Torah, just as what Scripture says constitutes Torah from God to Moses. That is what distinguishes wisdom from the Torah as it emerges in the context of rabbinic Judaism. To state the outcome in advance: we do not find the Torah in the Mishnah, and the Mishnah is not part of the Torah.

THE TORAH AS A PARTICULAR THING

The word Torah stands, first of all, for a concrete and material object, which people may use, or of which they may dispose. The Torah denotes in particular a Torah-scroll. What people do with a Torah-scroll is, mainly, read from it and study what is written in it, although, as we shall see, they may also buy or sell a Torah-scroll. Let us survey usages in which the word Torah, with or without a definite article, in context denotes a scroll as a concrete object. The Mishnah knows the word Torah joined to the word scroll, hence, Torah-scroll, a particular object, in two contexts. First of all, a Torah-scroll is an object used in the Temple or synagogue. Second, it is an object an individual may possess. The Torah-scroll as an object used in the Temple or synagogue occurs at M. Yoma 7:1; M. Sot. 7:7–8, both passages describing how a Torah-scroll is passed among authorities of ascending rank until it reaches the one who reads it. It is an object that a person may own, at M. Bes. 1:5; M. B.M. 4:9; and M. San. 2:4. At M. Bik. 3:12; M. B.M. 4:9 it is something one may buy or sell; at M. Sot. 7:7, it is handled. At M. San. 2:4, a king must write a Torah-scroll for his own purposes. M. Yeb. 16:7 knows that an individual routinely may have in his possession a staff, a cloak, and a Torah-scroll. "A town may sell scrolls and buy a Torah" (M. Meg. 3:1) can refer only to a Torah-scroll. It follows that "Torah" by itself may refer to a scroll.

"Torah" as a particular thing further occurs at M. Ta. 4:6, "He burned the Torah." "The Torah" refers to the Torah-scroll at M. Ber. 1:2, "One was reading in the Torah" (cf. also M. Ber. 2:1). "One begins [with a reading] in the Torah and concludes [with a reading in] the Prophets" bears the same sense (M. R.H. 4:6, with parallels at M. Meg. 4:1,2). "Reading in the Torah" further appears at M. Meg. 4:3,4,6. When, therefore, we ask what one does with such a concrete object, a Torah-scroll, the answer is clear. People read it; they study the words written in it.

None of these instances distinguishes between one kind of Torah and another. The notion of "the written Torah" as distinct from the oral one does not attach to the usage "Torah-scroll." That is, when "Torah-scroll" appears, it never contrasts with *Torah-not-in-a-scroll-but-memorized*. No secondary or abstract meaning attaches to "Torah-scroll."

THE TORAH AS REVELATION

When "the Torah" is used to denote a Torah-scroll, it normally connotes the value or authority not only of that particular scroll but also of what is in it, which is God's teachings, that is, revelation. The object is holy, not intrinsically, but because of what it contains. The word Torah in the Mishnah occasionally connotes divine revelation in Scripture. The meaning of "revelation" connoted by Torah occurs only twice when formulated in an explicit way as "the giving of the Torah." These are at M. Ta. 4:8 and M. Neg. 7:1. But the connotative meaning is common and well attested. So far as I can see, all instances in which "the Torah" or "Torah" in context connotes "revelation" refer to things written in Scripture as we know it. That is to say, when "the Torah" is explicitly cited, there always follows a citation from the written document.

"Torah" stands for a source of law at M. San. 8:5, "The Torah has said, 'Let him die unblemished. . . .'" The same usage occurs at M. Hal. 12:5, "The Torah has said. . . ." Along these same lines, "Therefore the Torah has assigned . . ." (M. Sot. 8:5) bears the same meaning. The sense is equivalent at M. Neg. 12:5, "The Torah has exhibited concern. . . ." "That [law] which is written in the Torah" occurs at M. Sheb. 10:3; M. Shab. 14:1; M. Pe. 6:2. "A whore of which the Torah speaks" occurs at M. Yeb. 6:5, with parallel references to M. Ket. 5:6; 9:1. At M. B.M. 7:1; M. B.B. 8:5, we find "that which is written in the Torah." Reference to what is mentioned in the Torah or listed there further occurs at M. B.B. 10:8; M. Shebu. 4:13; M. Hor. 1:1,3; M. Bekh. 7:2,5; M. Mak. 1:3. Along these same lines, we find the usage, "which is in the Torah," or, "written in . . . ," at M. Hal. 4:10; M. Bik. 1:3; M. Yeb. 6:2; M. Ned. 9:4; M. Qid. 3:12; M. San. 7:10; M. Shebu. 1:6; 7:1; M. Hor. 2:6; M. Zeb. 10:5; M. Hul. 12:5; M. Zab. 5:10. The usage is consistent throughout. "The teachings [words] of the Torah" (M. Sot. 7:5) seems to me to mean simply "the contents of Scripture."

Torah in the sense of a corpus of revealed doctrine occurs at M. Hag. 1:8, "essentials of Torah" referring to certain categories of legal study. One who says, "Torah does not come from Heaven" is excluded from the world to come (M. San. 10:1). This may mean that he says there is no such thing as revelation, or that *the Torah*, in particular, is not revealed from heaven. In context the latter seems more likely. When at M. Yoma 7:1; M. Sot. 7:7, we find a blessing on account of "*the Torah*, the Temple service," and so on, I am inclined to see use of this same meaning, that is, saying a blessing on account of the revealed doctrine (as distinct from the scroll, for instance). When, at M. Qid. 4:14, we are told that Abraham fulfilled "the entire Torah," the meaning is that he fulfilled the whole of divine revelation. "The Torah of Moses, your servant" appears at M. Yoma 3:8; 4:2; 6:2. The limited sense of "Torah of the priests" as the title of the Book of Leviticus is at M. Meg. 3:5; M. Men. 4:3. "Your Torah," that is, God's revelation, appears at M. Ber. 9:5, "They have nullified your Torah." A gentile refers to Israel's Torah as "Your Torah" at M. A.Z. 3:4. All of these uses of the word Torah understand the Torah in an established and familiar way. I do not think any Jew over the preceding half-millennium would have been puzzled by this usage.

TORAH AS A PARTICULAR ACT.
AS GENERIC

Among the several figurative or abstract meanings imputed to the word Torah in the Mishnah, the most interesting is "the study of Torah." To state matters in an impossible way, one "does *torah*" to Torah, that is, one *learns* or *studies torah* in the Torah. To state matters in the correct way, "in the Torah one acquires knowledge, in particular, of revelation." Accordingly, the meaning of revelation, source of revealed doctrine, carries in its wake an active verb-construction, *talmud torah*, study of revelation, as well as the secondary sense, for the word *torah*, of [revelation-] learning. And from this secondary sense, particular to the document and the act of learning that document, yet a tertiary sense emerges, *torah* as generic, that is, learning anything, not necessarily revelation.

Torah meaning study of Torah in particular, formulated explicitly as "study of Torah" (*talmud torah*), occurs at M. Pe. 1:1, as a matter subject to no fixed requirements. Disciples leave home for Torah-study (*talmud torah*) for a thirty-day period even without their wives' permission (M. Ket. 5:6). The same usage occurs at M. Ker. 6:9. In context, a disciple of a sage who "abandoned the Torah" has stopped learning, I should think (M. Hag. 1:7). But the sense of apostasy surely deserves a place as well. "Torah" in the sense of something one studies appears, without explicit reference to "study," at M. Sot. 3:4, "A man is obligated to *teach Torah* to his daughter." So too, at M. Qid. 4:14, "I should . . . *teach* my son only *Torah*." This exemplifies precisely the sense of *talmud torah*.

The Mishnah presents a few instances in which the word Torah entirely loses its capital T and ceases to refer to a particular object, on the one hand. But it also loses the connotation of revelation of God's will, on the other. Clear instances of such a generic use of *torah*, to mean "an act similar to the act performed when one studies [or gives] the Torah, hence an act of laying down a rule," occur in two passages. In these passages *torah* is a common noun, to be understood as taxon. "Torah" in the specific sense of a governing principle or rule in general occurs at M. Zeb. 11:1, "A single rule [*torah*] applies to all categories of sin-offering." So too we find at M. Sheb. 2:1, "You have put the rule [*torah*] into the hands of every individual [rather than applying a single rule to all]." Here, therefore, *torah* is generic and not particular.

"Torah" again in a generic sense, now of teaching or instruction, occurs at M. San. 11:2, "From there torah goes forth to all Israel." It is not possible to interpret the passage to mean that "the Torah"—God's revelation to Moses at Sinai—is what goes forth from the Hewn-stone Chamber. The meaning, "instruction, right decision" in context seems required. If that is so, then we have yet another instance in which *the Torah* loses all particularity and denotes a category or classification—in context, a decision of the highest standing. The generic usage then implies that The Torah has been used as the basis for a metaphor.

TORAH AS INDICATOR OF STATUS

The most striking step away from meaning by the word Torah or "the Torah," a particular thing or "something *like* a particular thing," occurs in the Mishnah's other principal sense of Torah. In this other sense, the word denotes a particular status. That status obtains either by itself or (more commonly) in contradistinction to another, lesser status. Specifically, the Mishnah will refer to a teaching that enjoys the standing or authority of the Torah, usually as distinct from a teaching that does not. The other, lesser teaching or rule rests upon the authority, not of what is written in the Torah, but of what is laid down by an (in the Mishnah) otherwise unidentified class or caste, "the scribes." The clearest statement of the distinction will have both "Torah" and "scribes" juxtaposed, as "the words of Torah . . . the words of scribes . . . ."

In the present context, I must stress, the meaning of "written To-rah" exhausts the intent of all the passages that refer to "Torah . . . scribes . . . ." Every instance understands that "the words of Torah" are *written* in Scripture, that is, derive from the Torah-scroll. So we stand well within the connotations attributed to the Torah-scroll as object, when we find this (evidently) secondary usage. Just as "the Torah" or "Torah" connotes "revealed doctrine," so the "standing" or "authority" of "the Torah" validates a particular rule or detail of the law. Accordingly, the connotative sense of the word "Torah" easily encompasses the present usage. But we do observe that although the usage has not become entirely abstract, "Torah" here has lost all con-crete and material relationship to a given book. For Torah here stands for something entirely abstract, namely, an imputed status. But the status imputed to a given rule or person in no way compares that rule or person to a book. So the abstraction is complete.

It remains to observe that the distinction at hand will serve as the foundation for one of the Babylonian Talmud's chief exegetical tools, its distinction between a rule enjoying the status of the Torah and one enjoying the lesser status of "the rabbis"—in context, equivalent to the scribes. As we shall see, in more than 450 passages, the Babylo-nian Talmud solves a problem (or creates one) by reference to the stated distinction. The Mishnah, for its part, knows the distinction full well. But what problems it proposes to solve by that distinction, or what difference the distinction really makes, are questions to which answers do not readily present themselves. To be sure, when the Talmud speaks of a rule resting upon authority of the Torah, it may associate that rule with what is found in the Mishnah as much as what is located in the written Torah. So the distinction between scrip-tural origin and rabbinical standing attracts more attention, I think, in the larger exegetical and hermeneutical labor of the authors of the Babylonian Talmud. So far as the Mishnah is concerned, it is a con-ventional and accepted distinction, but makes little difference overall.

In the present setting when the authors of the Mishnah speak of *the* Torah, they mean, first of all, "enjoying the status of a rule laid down in Scripture," as M. Ma. 2:7, "He does not eat [food in a certain cate-gory, on the strength of the authority of the law of] the Torah." The distinction between the level of highest authority, represented by the

Torah, and a lower level, represented by scribes, is found at M. San. 11:3, "A more strict rule applies [in the case of a law] deriving from the teachings of scribes than that deriving from the teachings of Torah . . . ." The same distinction occurs at M. Par. 11:4,11; and M. Yad. 3:2, "They do not deduce a logical argument by comparing teachings derived from the Torah to those derived from the scribes, and *vice versa*." The stated distinction is operative when the Mishnah's authors speak of "*the* Torah." Here they will mean, "On the authority of Scripture" as distinct from that of "scribes." The former sense is at M. Ma. 2:7, the latter, M. Or. 3:9. The sense of "proof deriving from a verse of Scripture" as against proof provided by mere reason appears at M. Sot. 5:2. This usage of "on the basis of the Torah" need not carry the implication of "in contradistinction to the rulings of sages." Certainly M. Ket. 3:7 does not imply such a contrast, nor do M. B.M. 2:10; 7:2; 7:8; M. Men. 10:5; M. Hul. 3:6; 8:4 and M. Miq. 6:7. In all these instances, the simple sense is, "on the basis of the authority of the Torah."

We do find two instances in which "the status of the Torah" defines the standing not of a given rule or law, hence of doctrine, but of persons. A "Torah person" (master, elder) is entirely outside the framework of meanings to be associated with the Torah as a scroll. Hence "Torah" no longer constitutes a document containing specific statements, teachings, rules, and the like. Applied to persons, "Torah" connotes status, not content or substance. In both instances of such a usage, all we know is that "Torah" connotes status for persons. But exactly how this is meant I am uncertain. Accordingly, I cannot say what "the Torah" means in the statement, "When R. Aqiba died, the honor [or glory] of the Torah came to an end" (M. Sot. 9:15). It could stand in the context of "study of Torah," with the sense that the "glory of the Torah, as something people learn, ended with the death of a particularly distinguished practitioner of Torah-study." But if that is the sense, I cannot demonstrate it in its immediate context. "Elders of Torah" in contrast to the "elders of the boors" appears at M. Qin. 3:6. The passage is a homiletical appendage. Here the meaning of "person in the status of Torah" seems legitimately imputed.

"Torah" as a classification of the same type as *misvah* (religious duty) occurs at M. Mak. 3:16. At M. Mak. 3:16, it is tacked on and external to the context. It seems to mean "study of Torah," but that sense is not decisively demanded by the context and may be an anachronism.

WRITTEN AND ORAL TORAH

The distinction between the oral Torah and the written Torah does not occur in the Mishnah, nor do the formulations *torah she-bikh tab* and *torah she-be'al peh*. No passage before us demands the meaning "not-written-down-Torah." None makes clear reference to a corpus of doctrine external to the written Torah, yet bearing *correlative* authority, and thus "*oral* Torah." Quite to the contrary. The contrast between the status of Torah ("words of Torah") and the status of authoritative-but-not-Torah ("teachings of scribes") precludes the conception of two Torahs of *equal* standing and authority, both deriving from God's revelation to Moses at Mount Sinai. Let me restate a simple, probative fact. Every Mishnah passage in which "the Torah" speaks, or in which people refer to "Torah" in either a denotative way or connotative setting, alludes to what is in the written Torah, either in general—as a status—or in particular, as a source of the given fact adduced in evidence.

Accordingly, not only does "the Torah" or "Torah" not denote the myth of the dual Torah. It also in no way even connotes it. Indeed, it forbids it! All the evidence of the Mishnah points to a single conclusion, in two parts. First, no one in the Mishnah has heard of any Torah revealed by God to Moses at Sinai except for the one in writing. Second, no one in the Mishnah imagines that the Mishnah, in particular, either derived from revelation at Sinai or even related to it. Whatever its authors thought the Mishnah was supposed to be, they never indicate that it enjoyed the status of Torah.

TORAH AS A SOURCE OF SALVATION

The Torah represents a source of salvation for Israel under one of two conditions. Either the individual, through study of the Torah and obedience to its teachings, achieves life after death, or the people Israel, through study of the Torah, is saved from this-worldly disasters of a national or local character or through the Torah draws nearer the coming of the Messiah and the eschatological rewards of the age to come. The conviction that the individual is saved through the Torah is amply expressed in Abot, where we shall see promises of direct encounter with God through study of the Torah. The nation at large in both Talmuds is promised salvation from all manner of troubles afflicting the community and salvation through the Messiah's coming. This salvation depends on loyalty to the Torah. Studying the Torah acts under some conditions like repetition of an incantation; and the Torah forms a powerful source of supernatural or magical power. But none of these convictions, broadly represented in both Talmuds and a few correlative documents, makes its appearance in the Mishnah. I know of no passage in which the Torah is other than a particular object, on the one side, or an indicator of status, on the other. Just as the Mishnah exhibits no myth of its own origins, so the framers of the document fail to endow with mythic character the Torah of Moses at Sinai. The scroll remains just that: a document, its teachings, their secondary effects and nothing more.

THE MISHNAH AND THE TORAH

When the authors of the Mishnah surveyed the landscape of Israelite writings down to their own time, they saw only Sinai, that is, what we now know as Scripture. Based on the documents they cite or mention, we can say with certainty that they knew the pentateuchal law. We may take for granted that they accepted as divine revelation also the Prophets and the Writings, to which they occasionally make reference. That they regarded as a single composition, that is, as revelation, the Torah, Prophets, and Writings appears from their references to *the Torah*, as a specific "book", and to a Torah-scroll. Accordingly, one important meaning associated with the word Torah, was concrete in the extreme. The Torah was a particular book or sets of books, regarded as holy, revealed to Moses at Sinai. That fact presents no surprise, since the Torah-scroll(s) had existed, it is generally assumed, for many centuries before the closure of the Mishnah in 200 C.E.

What is surprising is that everything from the formation of the canon of the Torah to their own day seems to have proved null in their eyes. Between the Mishnah and Mount Sinai lay a vast, empty plain. From the perspective of the Torah-myth as they must have known it, from Moses and the prophets, to before Judah the Patriarch, lay a great wasteland. So the concrete and physical meaning attaching to the word Torah, that is, *the Torah*, the Torah revealed by God to Moses at Mount Sinai (including the books of the Prophets and the Writings), bore a contrary implication. Beyond *The Torah* there was no *torah*. Besides the Pentateuch, Prophets, and Writings, not only did no physical scroll deserve veneration, but no corpus of writings demanded obedience. So the very limited sense in which the words *the Torah* were used passed a stern judgment upon everything else, all the other writings that we know circulated widely, in which other Jews alleged that God had spoken and said "these things."

The range of the excluded possibilities that other Jews explored demands no survey. It includes everything, not only the Gospels (by 200 C.E. long since in the hands of outsiders), but secret books, history books, psalms, wisdom writings, rejected works of prophecy—everything excluded from any biblical canon by whoever determined there should be a canon. If the library of the Essenes at Qumran tells us what might have been, then we must regard as remarkably impoverished the (imaginary) library that would have served the authors of the Mishnah: the Book of Books, but nothing else. We seldom see so stern, so austere a vision of what commands the status of holy revelation among Judaisms over time. The tastes of the Mishnah's authors express a kind of literary iconoclasm, but with a difference. The literary icons did survive in the churches of Christendom. But in their own society and sacred setting, the judgment of Mishnah's authors would prevail from its time to ours. Nothing in the Judaisms of the heritage from the Hebrew Scripture's time to the Mishnah's day would survive the implacable rejection of the framers of the Mishnah, unless under Christian auspices or buried in caves. So when we take up that first and simplest meaning associated with the word Torah, "*The* Torah," we confront a stunning judgment: this and nothing else, this alone, this thing alone of its kind and no other thing of similar kind.

We confront more than a closing off of old possibilities, ancient claims to the status of revelation. For, at the other end, out of *the Torah* as a particular thing, a collection of books, would emerge a new and remarkably varied set of meanings. Possibilities first generated by the fundamental meaning imputed to the word Torah would demand realization. How so? Once the choice for the denotative meaning of *the Torah* became canonical in the narrowest possible sense, the ranges of connotative meaning imputed to the Torah stretched forth to an endless horizon. So the one concrete meaning made possible many abstract ones, all related to that single starting point. Only at the end shall we clearly grasp, in a single tableau, the entire vista of possibilities. To begin with, it suffices to note that the Mishnah's theory of the Torah not only closed, but also opened, many paths.

2

Abot:
From the Torah to Torah

TOWARD A THEORY OF THE MISHNAH

Tractate Abot ("Founders") presents sayings assigned to authorities from "the Men of the Great Assembly," otherwise unidentified, to sages of the generation beyond Judah the Patriarch. These latter figures are assumed to have lived in the early part of the third century, so Abot will have come to closure no earlier than 250. The prominence of the term *Torah* in the tractate demands that we review the entire document and delineate not only the several usages, but also the larger theory of the matter. This verbatim survey also points to what we do not find.

Abot provides no account of the origin and authority of the Mishnah as a finished document. The framers make no explicit reference to the Mishnah at all. But there is an implicit message. For when they speak about *Torah*, their composition encompasses sayings of principal figures of the Mishnah. It must follow that the authors or compilers see a connection between the *Torah*, specifically revelation of God to Moses at Mount Sinai, and *the authorities of the contents of* the Mishnah, that is, things said by Mishnah's sages. The chain of tradition from Sinai extends through unknown and legendary figures, such as the Men of the Great Assembly, to known and familiar ones, such as Shammai, Hillel, and their disciples and heirs. Hillel's successors comprise both his family, through his son and grandson—hence the patriarchal house of Judah itself—and his disciples, through Yohanan ben Zakkai. Henceforward, then, we find such well-known and commonplace names as Joshua, Eliezer, Aqiba, Meir, Judah, Simeon, and the like.

This means that the important authorities of the Mishnah are placed in a direct line with Sinai. That should also carry the implication that their opinions, assembled in the Mishnah, enjoy the status of revelation. But Abot does not specify the Mishnah as the principal vehicle for the transmission of the Torah of Sinai. The Mishnah is not represented as part of the one whole Torah of Moses, our rabbi. As I shall point out, that vehicle, for Abot, proves personal and human, namely, the sage himself. True, the sage is not called a Torah, but neither is the Mishnah. The *status* of Torah appears to encompass the sage. But the metaphor of the Torah does not envelop the sages' book, the Mishnah. My guess is, as I noted earlier, that for Abot the Mishnah does not present a critical problem of apologetics. Why not? Because the Mishnah for Abot—fifty years after the Mishnah appeared—has not yet gained the standing of a completed and autonomous document (whether orally published or otherwise). The Mishnah still forms a stage in the process of tradition in a chain made up of human links, that is, sages, and not of documentary ones, that is, completed books.

The importance of tractate Abot to our inquiry requires specification. The claim that the Mishnah derives from Sinai and forms the oral part of "the one whole Torah of Moses our rabbi" generally refers back to the tractate at hand. People find that assertion at Abot 1:1–18. In fact, as we shall now see, Abot disappoints those who seek in its apophthegms the source for the opinion that, first, two Torahs came from Sinai, and, second, the Mishnah and documents flowing from it constitute one of those two Torahs. The document knows that it is important to study Torah. It nowhere cites—e.g., as a proof-text—a passage of the Mishnah or in some other way represents the Mishnah as Torah. The Mishnah as a whole is unknown to Abot; in it, not a single line of the other sixty-two tractates merits even remote allusion. Indeed, as an apologetic in behalf of the Mishnah, the tractate at hand performs remarkably slight service. For, as I have stressed, its connection to the Mishnah lies only in the names of sages appearing both in Abot and in other tractates of the Mishnah. But the teachings that sages deliver in Abot—their wise sayings—are not represented as Torah. And those sayings do not square with anything stated by the same sages anywhere else in the Mishnah. So Abot demonstrates importantly something other than what has been conventionally deduced from it. Still, of all the documents of formative Judaism, the tractate at hand proves the most important for our inquiry. How so?

Abot is the sole complete tractate, above all others, devoted to study of Torah.

At the outset, we shall review the relevant chapters of the entire document, so, that, in the sections to follow, we may merely allude briefly to the unit under discussion. Tractate Abot, chapters 1—4, follow. Chapter 5, simply a set of number constructions, diverges so radically that we bypass it here. Though some allusions to "sages" occur, and chapter 5 does provide a repertoire of statements fully consonant with the values or virtues associated with *Torah*, meaning sagacity and its disciplines (e.g., a sage vs. a clod), nonetheless the issue of "the Torah" or of "Torah" as a doctrine or even *torah* as a type of activity or generic does not come to the fore. A few brief comments highlight some of the literary traits of chapters 1—4.

1:1–18

I. A. Moses received Torah at Sinai and handed it on to Joshua, Joshua to elders, and elders to prophets.

B. And prophets handed it on to the Men of the Great Assembly.

C. They said three things:
(1) "Be prudent in judgment.
(2) "Raise up many disciples.
(3) "Make a fence for the Torah"[M. 1:1].

II. A. Simeon the Righteous was one of the last survivors of the great assembly.

B. He would say: "On three things does the world stand:
(1) "On the Torah,
(2) "and on the Temple service,
(3) "and on deeds of loving kindness" [M. 1:2].

III. A. Antigonos of Sokho received [the Torah] from Simeon the Righteous.

B. He would say,
(1) "Do not be like servants who serve the master on condition of receiving a reward,
(2) "but [be] like servants who serve the master not on condition of receiving a reward.
(3) "And let the fear of Heaven be upon you" [M. 1:3].

I. A. Yose b. Yoezer of Seredah and Yose b. Yohanan of Jerusalem received [it] from them.

B. Yose b. Yoezer says,
(1) "Let your house be a gathering place for sages.

        (2) "And wallow in the dust of their feet.

        (3) "And drink in their words with gusto" [M. 1:4].

    A. Yose b. Yohanan of Jerusalem says,

        (1) "Let your house be wide open.

        (2) "And seat the poor at your table

        ["make . . . members of your household"].

        (3) "And don't talk too much with women."

    B. (He spoke of a man's wife, all the more so is the rule to be applied to the wife of one's fellow. In this regard did sages say, "So long as a man talks too much with a woman, (1) he brings trouble on himself, (2) wastes time better spent on studying Torah, and (3) ends up an heir of Gehenna.") [M. 1:5]

II. A. Joshua b. Perahiah and Nittai the Arbelite received [it] from them.

    B. Joshua b. Perahiah says,

        (1) "Set up a master for yourself.

        (2) "And give yourself a fellow-disciple.

        (3) "And give everybody the benefit of the doubt" [M. 1:6].

    A. Nittai the Arbelite says,

        (1) "Keep away from a bad neighbor.

        (2) "And don't get involved with a bad man.

        (3) "And don't give up hope of retribution" [M. 1:7].

III. A. Judah b. Tabbai and Simeon b. Shatah received [it] from them.

    B. Judah b. Tabbai says,

        (1) "Don't make yourself like one of those who make advocacy before judges [while you yourself are judging a case].

        (2) "And when the litigants stand before you, regard them as guilty.

        (3) "But when they leave you, regard them as acquitted, (when they have accepted your judgment)"[M. 1:8].

    A. Simeon b. Shatah says.

        (1) "Examine the witnesses with great care.

        (2) "And watch what you say,

        (3) "lest they learn from what you say how to lie" [M. 1:9].

IV. A. Shemaiah and Abtalion received [it] from them.

    B. Shemaiah says,

        (1) "Love work.

        (2) "Hate authority.

        (3) "Don't get friendly with the government" [M. 1:10].

    A. Abtalion says,
- (1) "Sages, watch what you say,
  "Lest you become liable to the punishment of exile, and go into exile to a place of bad water, and disciples who follow drink the bad water and die, and the name of Heaven be thereby profaned" [M.1:11].

V. A. Hillel and Shammai received [it] from them.

    B. Hillel says,
- (1) "Be disciples of Aaron,
- (2) "loving peace and pursuing grace,
- (3) "loving people and drawing them near to the Torah" [M. 1:12].

    A. He would say [in Aramaic],
- (1) "A name made great is a name destroyed.
- (2) "And one who does not add subtracts.
- (3) "And who does not learn is liable to death.
- (4) "And the one who uses the crown passes away" [M. 1:13].

    A. He would say,
- (1) "If I am not for myself, who is for me?
- (2) "And when I am for myself, what am I?
- (3) "And if not now, when?" [M. 1:14]

    A. Shammai says,
- (1) "Make your learning of Torah a fixed obligation.
- (2) "Say little and do much.
- (3) "Greet everybody cheerfully" [M. 1:15].

I. A. Rabban Gamaliel says,
- (1) "Set up a master for yourself.
- (2) "Avoid doubt.
- (3) "Don't tithe by too much guesswork" [M. 1:16].

II. A. Simeon his son says,
- (1) "All my life I grew up among the sages, and I found nothing better for a person [the body] than silence.
- (2) "And not the learning is the thing, but the doing.
- (3) "And whoever talks too much causes sin" [M. 1:17].

III. A. Rabban Simeon b. Gamaliel says, "On three things does the world stand:
- (1) "on justice,
- (2) "on truth,
- (3) "and on peace,

    B. "as it is said, *Execute the judgment of truth and peace in your gates* (Zech. 8:16)" [M. 1:18].

The formal traits are clear: *name* + *attributive* + *three sayings*. But the formal pattern announced at M. 1:1 does not predominate throughout, and the introduction of the pairs, M. 1:4ff., after the singletons beginning with M. 1:1B's "Men of the Great Assembly," starts a new unit as well. Since the formal pattern involving pairs with three sayings each is well established, the set of *says in Hillel's name* is jarring. In this regard, M. 1:11 and M. 1:12B constitute a formal pair, which carefully ignore the otherwise paramount preference. It is only at M. 1:14 that the expected trait reappears, and then, as we see, it runs on to the end. I am inclined to think that M. 1:12A is best carried forward at M. 1:14, with what is in between a lengthy interpolation. I do not know how to make sense of Abtalion. The end of the pairs is not without its problems, since M. 1:17 and M. 1:18 supply two distinct continuations to M. 1:16. M. 1:1; 1:6; 1:8–9 deal with advice to judges. Sayings for disciples are at M. 1:1, 3, 4, 6, 11, 13, 15, 16, 17; and the rest are a miscellany of good advice.

2:1

I.   A. Rabbi says, "What is the straight path which a person should choose for himself? Whatever is an ornament to the one who follows it, and an ornament in the view of others.

II.   B. "Be meticulous in a small religious duty as in a large one, for you do not know what sort of reward is coming for any of the various religious duties.

C. "And reckon with the loss [required] in carrying out a religious duty against the reward for doing it,

D. "and the reward for committing a transgression against the loss for doing it.

III.   E. "And keep your eye on three things, so you will not come into the clutches of transgression:

F. "Know what is above you:

G. "(1)An eye which sees, and (2) an ear which hears, and (3) all your actions written down in a book."

2:2–7

I.   A. Rabban Gamaliel, son of R. Judah, the Patriarch, says, "Fitting is learning in Torah along with a craft, for the labor put into the two of them makes one forget sin.

B. "And all learning of Torah which is not joined with labor is destined to be null and causes sin.

II.   C. "And all who work with the community—let them work with them for the sake of Heaven.

       D. "For the merit of their fathers strengthens them, and the righteousness which they do stands forever.

       E. "And as for you, I credit you with a great reward, as if you had done [all of the work required by the community]" [M. 2:2].

III.   A. "Be wary of the government, for they get friendly with a person only for their own convenience.

       B. "They look like friends when it is to their benefit, but they do not stand by a person when he is in need" [M. 2:3].

IV.   A. He would say, "Make his wishes your own wishes, so that he will make your wishes his wishes.

       B. "Put aside your wishes on account of his wishes, so that he will put aside the wishes of other people in favor of your wishes."

I.   C. Hillel says, "Do not walk out on the community.

II.   D. "And do not have confidence in yourself until the day you die.

III.   E. "And do not judge your fellow until you are in his place.

IV.   F. "And do not say anything which cannot be heard, for in the end it will be heard.

V.   G. "And do not say, 'When I have time, I shall study,' for you may never have time" [M. 2:4].

       A. He would say, (1) "A coarse person will never fear sin, (2) nor will an *am ha'ares* ever be pious, (3) nor will a shy person learn, (4) nor will an intolerant person teach, (5) nor will anyone too busy in business get wise.

       B. "In a place in which there are no men, try to act like a man" [M. 2:5].

       A. Also he saw a skull floating on the water and said to it, "Because you drowned others, they drowned you, and in the end those who drowned you will be drowned" [M. 2:6].

       A. He would say, "(1) Lots of meat, lots of worms; (2) lots of property, lots of worries; (3) lots of women, lots of witchcraft; (4) lots of slave-girls, lots of lust; (5) lots of slave-boys, lots of robbery.

       B. "(6) Lots of Torah, lots of life; (7) lots of discipleship, lots of wisdom; (8) lots of counsel, lots of understanding; (9) lots of righteousness, lots of peace."

       C. "[If] one has gotten a good name, he has gotten it for himself.

D. "[If] he has gotten teachings of Torah, he has gotten himself
life eternal" [M. 2:7].

The two sons of Rabbi (= Judah the Patriarch), Gamaliel and
Hillel, appear before us. The former has four sayings, M. 2:2A–B,
C–D (+ E, which is meaningless); M. 2:3; and M. 2:4A–B. Perhaps M. 2:2E is part of a fifth entry, but I cannot imagine what it
might have been. Hillel has groups of sayings, five at M. 2:4C–G;
five at M. 2:5; two singletons, M. 2:5B and 2:6, and then nine at M.
2:6A–B.

2:8–14

A. Rabban Yohanan b. Zakkai received [it] from Hillel and
Shammai.
B. He would say,
"(1) If you have learned much Torah, (2) do not puff yourself
up on that account, (3) for it was for that purpose that you
were created."
C. He had five disciples, and these are they: R. Eliezer b.
Hyrcanus, R. Joshua b. Hananiah, R. Yose the priest, R.
Simeon b. Netanel, and R. Eleazar b. Arakh.
D. He would list their good qualities:
E. R. Eliezer b. Hyrcanus: A plastered well, which does not
lose a drop of water.
F. R. Joshua: Happy is the one who gave birth to him.
G. R. Yose: A pious man.
H. R. Simeon b. Netanel: A man who fears sin.
I. And R. Eleazar b. Arakh: A surging spring.
J. He would say, "If all the sages of Israel were on one side of
the scale and R. Eliezer b. Hyrcanus on the other, he would
outweigh all of them."
K. Abba Saul says in his name, "If all of the sages of Israel were
on one side of the scale, and R. Eliezer b. Hyrcanus was also
with them, and R. Eleazar [b. Arakh] were on the other side,
he would outweigh all of them" [M. 2:8].
A. He said to them, "Go and see what is the straight path to
which someone should stick."
B. R. Eliezer says, "A generous spirit."
C. R. Joshua says, "A good friend."
D. R. Yose says, "A good neighbor."
E. R. Simeon says, "Foresight."
F. R. Eleazar says, "Good will."

G. He said to them, "I prefer the opinion of R. Eleazar b. Arakh, because in what he says is included everything you say."

H. He said to them, "Go out and see what is the bad road, which someone should avoid."

I. R. Eliezer says, "Envy,"

J. R. Joshua says, "A good friend."

K. R. Yose says, "A bad neighbor."

L. R. Simeon says, "Reneging on a loan."

M. (All the same is a loan owed to a human being and a loan owed to the Omnipresent, blessed be he, as it is said, *The wicked borrows and does not pay back, but the righteous person deals graciously and hands over [what he owes]* [Ps. 37:21].)

N. R. Eleazar says, "Bad will."

O. He said to them, "I prefer the opinion of R. Eleazar b. Arakh, because in what he says is included everything you say" [M. 2:9].

A. They [each] said three things.

B. R. Eliezer says, "(1) Let the respect owing to your fellow be as precious to you as the respect owing to you yourself.

C. "(2) And don't be easy to anger.

D. "(3) And repent one day before you die.

E. "And (1) warm yourself by the fire of the sages, but be careful of their coals, so you don't get burned.

F. "(2) For their bite is the bite of a fox, and their sting is the sting of a scorpion, and their hiss is like the hiss of a snake.

G. "(3) And everything they say is like fiery coals" [M. 2:10].

A. R. Joshua says, "(1) Envy, (2) desire of bad things, and (3) hatred for people push a person out of the world" [M. 2:11].

A. R. Yose says, "(1) Let your fellow's money be as precious to you as your own.

B. "And (2) get yourself ready to learn Torah,

C. "for it does not come as an inheritance to you.

D. "And (3) may everything you do be for the sake of Heaven" [M. 2:12].

A. R. Simeon says, "(1) Be meticulous about the recitation of the *Shema* and the Prayer.

B. "And (2) when you pray, don't treat your praying as a matter of routine.

C. "But let it be a [plea for] mercy and supplications before the Omnipresent, blessed be he.

D. "As it is said, *For he is gracious and full of compassion, slow to anger and full of mercy, and repents of the evil* (Joel 2:13).

E. "(3) And never be evil in your own eyes" [M. 2:13].

A. R. Eleazar says, "(1) Be constant in learning of Torah.

B. "(2) And know what to reply to a heretic.

C. "(3) And know before whom you work,

D. "for your employer can be depended upon to pay your wages for what you can do" [M. 2:14].

Yohanan b. Zakkai has the expected three sayings; he could as well have been located in chapter 1. M. 2:6 begins a long sequence of units, three in all, in which Eleazar b. Arakh is set as the climax. If this were not formally obvious, Abba Saul's saying would have made the point anyhow. At each point in Eleazar's triplet (M. 2:8D–K; M. 2:9, and M. 2:10–14), Eleazar is placed at the end and given the best saying. M. 2:10A is misleading. Eliezer has two sets of three sayings, as indicated. But Joshua gets three sayings only by stretching things out. M. 2:13C–D constitutes a major interpolation, extending M. 2:12B, and M. 2:14D does the same. In all, we have a remarkably well constructed unit for Yohanan and his disciples.

2:15–16

A. R. Tarfon says, "(1) The day is short, (2) the work formidable, (3) the workers lazy, (4) the wages high, (5) the employer impatient" [M. 2:15].

I. A. He would say, "It's not your job to finish the work, but you're not free to walk away from it.

II. B. "If you have learned much Torah, they will give you a good reward.

III. C. "And your employer can be depended upon to pay your wages for what you do.

D. "And know what sort of reward is going to be given to the righteous in the coming time" [M. 2:16].

M. 2:16D seems out of phase with the foregoing and seems as a development of C. But M. 2:16C goes over the ground of M. 2:14D, so that may be the culprit.

Seventeen sages are presented in chapter 3, some of them with sizable and well-constructed sets of sayings in disciplined form, others give miscellaneous and even scarcely coherent ones. There are some marks of secondary development and expansion, which are fairly easy to discern, e.g., at M. 3:1C–E for M. 3:1A–B. Some sayings tend to go over a single theme, e.g., the presence of God where Torah is studied, at M. 3:2; 3:3; 3:6. About half of the sayings deal with Torah-learning, M. 3:2, 3, 5, 6, 8, 9–10 (works more important than learning), 17 (proper conduct is a prerequisite of learning, and vice versa). It cannot be said, however, that the chapter as a whole simply lays out sayings on the importance of Torah-study, and some of the moral sayings criticize Torah-study by itself, i.e., when it is not joined to right action.

3:1

A. Aqabiah b. Mehallalel says, "Reflect upon three things and you will not fall into the clutches of transgression:

B. "Know (1) from whence you come, (2) whither you are going, and (3) before whom you are going to have to give a full account of yourself.

C. *"From whence do you come?* From a putrid drop.

D. *"Whither are you going?* To a place of dust, worms and maggots.

E. *"And before whom are you going to give a full account of yourself?* Before the King of kings of kings, the Holy One, blessed be he."

3:2–3

A. R. Hananiah, Prefect of the Priests, says, "Pray for the welfare of the government.

B. "For if it were not for fear of it, one man would swallow his fellow alive."

C. R. Hananiah b. Teradion says, "[If] two sit together and between them do not pass teachings of Torah, lo, this is a *seat of the scornful,*

D. "as it is said, *Nor sits in the seat of the scornful* (Ps. 1:1).

E. "But two who are sitting, and words of Torah do pass between them—the Presence is with them,

F. "as it is said, *Then they that feared the Lord spoke with one another, and the Lord hearkened and heard, and a book of remembrance was written before him, for them that feared the Lord and gave thought to His name* (Mal. 3:16)."

G. I know that this applies to two.

H. How do I know that even if a single person sits and works on

Torah, the Holy One, blessed be He, sets aside a reward for him?

I. "As it is said, *Let him sit alone and keep silent, because he has laid it upon him* (Lam. 3:28)" [M. 3:2].

A. R. Simeon says, "Three who ate at a single table and did not talk about teachings of Torah while at that table are as though they ate from *dead sacrifices* (Ps. 106:28),

B. "as it is said, *For all tables are full of vomit and filthiness [if they are] without God* (Is. 28:8).

C. "But three who ate at a single table and did talk about teachings of Torah at that table are as if they ate at the table of the Omnipresent, blessed is he,

D. "as it is said, *And he said to me, This is the table that is before the Lord* (Ez. 41:22)" [M. 3:3].

Hananiah b. Teradion and Simeon cover the same ground, which I assume accounts for the juxtaposition of their sayings.

3:4–6

A. R. Hananiah b. Hakhinai says, "(1) He who gets up at night, and (2) he who walks around by himself, and (3) he who turns his desire to emptiness—lo, this person is liable for his life" [M. 3:4].

A. R. Nehunia b. Haqqaneh says, "From whoever accepts upon himself the yoke of Torah, do they remove the yoke of the state and the yoke of hard labor.

B. "And upon whoever removes from himself the yoke of the Torah do they lay the yoke of the state and the yoke of hard labor" [M. 3:5].

A. R. Halafta of Kefar Hananiah says, "Among ten who sit and work hard on Torah, the Presence comes to rest,

B. "as it is said, *God stands in the congregation of God* (Ps. 82:1).

C. "And how do we know that the same is so even of five? *For it is said, And he has founded his group upon the earth* (Am. 9:6).

D. "And how do we know that this is so even of three? Since it is said, *And he judges among the judges* (Ps. 82:1).

E. "And how do we know that this is so even of two? Because it is said, *Then they that feared the Lord spoke with one another, and the Lord hearkened and heard* (Mal. 3:16).

F. "And how do we know that this is so even of one? Since it is said, *In every place where I record my name I will come to you and I will bless you* (Ex. 20:24)" [M. 3:6].

Halafta, M. 3:6, appears to return to the notion of M. 3:2–3, now with Torah-study at the center.

3:7–8

A. R. Eleazar of Bartota says, "Give him what is his, for you and yours are his.

B. "For so does it say about David, *For all things come of you, and of your own have we given you* (1 Chron. 29:14)."

C. R. Simeon says, "He who is going along the way and repeating [his Torah-tradition] but interrupts his repetition and says, 'How beautiful is that tree! How beautiful is that ploughed field!' Scripture reckons it to him as if he has become liable for his life" [M. 3:7].

A. R. Dosetai b. R. Yannai in the name of R. Meir says, "Whoever forgets a single thing from what he has learned—Scripture reckons it to him as if he has become liable for his life,

B. "as it is said, *Only take heed to yourself and keep your soul diligently, lest you forget the words which your eyes saw* (Deut. 4:9)."

C. Is it possible that this is so even if his learning became too much for him?

D. Scripture says, *Lest they depart from your heart all the days of your life* (Deut. 4:9).

E. Thus he becomes liable for his life only when he will sit down and actually remove [his learning] from his own heart [M. 3:8].

3:9–10

I. A. R. Hanina b. Dosa says, "For anyone whose fear of sin takes precedence over his wisdom, his wisdom will endure.

B. "And for anyone whose wisdom takes precedence over his fear of sin, his wisdom will not endure."

II. C. He would say, "Anyone whose deeds are more than his wisdom—his wisdom will endure.

D. "And anyone whose wisdom is more than his deeds—his wisdom will not endure" [M. 3:9].

III. A. He would say, "Anyone in whom people take pleasure—the Omnipresent takes pleasure.

B. "And anyone in whom people do not take pleasure, the Omnipresent does not take pleasure."

C. R. Dosa b. Harkinas says, "(1) Sleeping late in the morning, (2) drinking wine at noon, (3) chatting with children, and (4) attending the synagogues of the ignorant drive a man out of the world" [M. 3:10].

3:11–16

A. R. Eleazar the Modite says, "(1) He who treats Holy Things as secular, (2) he who despises the appointed times, (3) he who humiliates his fellow in public, (4) he who removes the signs of the covenant of Abraham, our father, (may he rest in peace), and (5) he who exposes aspects of the Torah not in accord with the law,

B. "even though he has in hand learning in Torah and good deeds, will have no share in the world to come" [M. 3:11].

A. R. Ishmael says, "(1) Be quick [in service] to a superior, (2) efficient in service [to the state], and (3) receive everybody with joy" [M. 3:12].

A. R. Aqiba says, "(1) Laughter and lightheadedness turn lewdness into a habit.

B. "(2) Tradition is a fence for the Torah.

C. "(3) Tithes are a fence for wealth.

D. "(4) Vows are a fence for abstinence.

E. "(5) A fence for wisdom is silence" [M. 3:13].

I. A. He would say, "Precious is the human being, who was created in the image [of God].

B. "It was an act of still greater love that it was made known to him that he was created in the image [of God],

C. "as it is said, *For in the image of God he made man* (Gen. 9:6).

II. D. "Precious are Israelites, who are called children to the Omnipresent.

E. "It was an act of still greater love that it was made known to them that they were called children to the Omnipresent,

F. "as it is said, *You are the children of the Lord your God* (Deut. 14:1).

III. G. "Precious are Israelites, to whom was given the precious thing.

H. "It was an act of still greater love that it was made known to them that to them was given that precious thing with which the world was made,

I.   I. "as it is said, *For I give you a good doctrine. Do not forsake my Torah* (Prov. 4:2) [M. 3:14].

I.   A. "Everything is foreseen, but free choice is given.

II.   B. "In goodness the world is judged.

III.   C. "And all is in accord with the abundance of deed[s]" [M. 3:15].

      A. He would say, "(1) All is handed over as a pledge,

      B. "(2) and a net is cast over all the living.

      C. "(3) The store is open, (4) the storekeeper gives credit, (5) the account-book is open, and (6) the hand is writing.

      D. "(1) Whoever wants to borrow may come and borrow.

      E. "(2) The charity-collectors go around every day and collect from man whether he knows it or not.

      F. "(3) And they have grounds for what they do.

      G. "(4) And the judgment is a true judgment.

      H. "(5) And everything is ready for the meal" [M. 3:16].

3:17–18

I.   A. R. Eleazar b. Azariah says, "If there is no learning of Torah, there is no proper conduct.

      B. "If there is no proper conduct, there is no learning in Torah.

II.   C. "If there is no wisdom, there is no reverence.

      D. "If there is no reverence, there is no wisdom.

III.   E. "If there is no understanding, there is no knowledge.

      F. "If there is no knowledge, there is no understanding.

IV.   G. "If there is no sustenance, there is no Torah-learning.

      H. "If there is no Torah-learning, there is no sustenance."

I.   I. He would say, "Anyone whose wisdom is greater than his deeds—to what is he to be likened? To a tree with abundant foliage, but few roots.

      J. "When the winds come, they will uproot it and blow it down,

      K. "as it is said, *He shall be like a tamarisk in the desert and shall not see when good comes, but shall inhabit the parched places in the wilderness* (Jer. 17:6).

II.   L. "But anyone whose deeds are greater than his wisdom—to what is he to be likened? To a tree with little foliage but abundant roots.

      M. "For even if all the winds in the world come and blast at it, they will not move it from its place,

      N. "as it is said, *He shall be as a tree planted by the waters, and that spreads out its roots by the river, and shall not fear when heat comes, and his leaf shall be green, and shall not be careful in the year of drought, neither shall cease from yielding fruit* (Jer. 17:8)." [M. 3:17].

A. R. Eleazar Hisma says, "The laws of bird-offerings and the absolution of vows—they are indeed the essentials of the Torah.

B. "Calculations of the equinoxes and reckoning the numerical value of letters are the savories of wisdom" [M. 3:18].

Twenty-five sages are represented in chapter 4, the first group, Ushans, ca. 140–70, M. 4:1–19, the second, their successors, ca. 170–200, M. 4:20–22. Some of the sayings are sizable and well crafted, e.g., Ben Zoma's M. 4:1; others are brief and miscellaneous. Eliezer Haqqappar concludes the whole with a strikingly expansive construction, larger and more substantial than anything else before us. Since what follows in chapter 5 are long sequences of number constructions, lacking named authorities, it may be that Eliezer's set is meant to mark the completion of the "tractate" at some early stage in its formation or agglutination.

4:1–3

I. A. Ben Zoma says, "Who is a sage? He who learns from everybody,

 B. "as it is said, *From all my teachers I have gotten understanding* (Ps. 119:99).

II. C. "Who is strong? He who overcomes his desire,

 D. "as it is said, *He who is slow to anger is better than the mighty, and he who rules his spirit than he who takes a city* (Prov. 16:32).

III. E. "Who is rich? He who is happy in what he has,

 F. "as it is said, *When you eat the labor of your hands, happy will you be, and it will go well with you* (Ps. 128:2).

 G. ("Happy will you be—in this world, and it will go well with you—in the world to come.")

IV. H. "Who is honored? He who honors everybody,

 I. "as it is said, *For those who honor me I shall honor, and they who despise me will be treated as of no account* (1 Sam. 2:30)" [M. 4:1].

A. Ben Azzai says, "Run after the most minor religious duty as after the most important, and flee from transgression.

B. "For doing one religious duty draws in its wake doing yet another, and doing one transgression draws in its wake doing yet another.

C. "For the reward of doing a religious duty is a religious duty, and the reward of doing a transgression is a transgression" [M. 4:2].

A. He would say, "Do not despise anybody and do not treat anything as unlikely.

B. "For you have no one who does not have his time, and you have nothing which does not have its place" [M. 4:3].

Both authorities have statements of paradox, as at M. 4:3. Ben Zoma hears a gloss at M. 4:1G, and Ben Azzai's saying is given a double amplification, M. 4:2B, C.

4:4–8

A. R. Levitas of Yabneh says, "Be exceedingly humble, for the hope of humanity is the worm."

B. R. Yohanan b. Beroqa says, "Whoever secretly treats the Name of Heaven as profane publicly pays the price.

C. "All the same are the one who does so inadvertently and the one who does so deliberately, when it comes to treating the Name of Heaven as profane" [M. 4:4].

A. R. Ishmael, his son, says, "He who learns so as to teach —they give him a chance to learn and to teach.

B. "He who learns so as to carry out his teachings—they give him a chance to learn, to teach, to keep, and to do."

C. R. Sadoq says, "Do not make [Torah-teachings] a crown in which to glorify yourself or a spade with which to dig.

D. (So did Hillel say [M. 1:13], "He who uses the crown perishes.")

E. "Thus have you learned: Whoever derives worldly benefit from teachings of Torah takes his life out of this world" [M. 4:5].

A. R. Yose says, "Whoever honors the Torah is himself honored by people.

B. "And whoever disgraces the Torah is himself disgraced by people" [M. 4:6].

A. R. Ishmael, his son, says, "He who avoids serving as a judge breaks off the power of enmity, robbery, and false swearing.

B. "And he who is arrogant about making decisions is a fool, evil, and prideful" [M. 4:7].

A. He would say, "Do not serve as a judge by yourself, for there is only One who serves as a judge all alone.

B. "And do not say, 'Accept my opinion,'

C. "for they have the choice in that matter, not you" [M. 4:8].

4:9–14

A. R. Yonatan says, "Whoever keeps the Torah in poverty will in the end keep it in wealth.

B. "And whoever treats the Torah as nothing when he is wealthy in the end will treat it as nothing when he is poor" [M. 4:9].

A. R. Meir says, "Keep your business to a minimum and make your business Torah.

B. "And be humble before everybody.

C. "And if you treat the Torah as nothing, you will have many treating you as nothing.

D. "And if you have labored in Torah, [the Torah] has a great reward to give you" [M. 4:10].

A. R. Eliezer b. Jacob says, "He who does even a single religious duty gets himself a good advocate.

B. "He who does even a single transgression gets himself a powerful prosecutor.

C. "Penitence and good deeds are like a shield against punishment."

D. R. Yohanan Hassandelar says, "Any gathering which is for the sake of Heaven is going to endure.

E. "And any which is not for the sake of Heaven is not going to endure" [M. 4:11].

A. R. Eleazar b. Shammua says, "The honor owing to your disciple should be as precious to you as yours,

B. "And the honor owing to your fellow should be like the reverence owing to your master.

C. "And the reverence owing to your master should be like the awe owing to Heaven" [M. 4:12].

A. R. Judah says, "Be meticulous about learning,

B. "for error in learning leads to deliberate [violation of the Torah]."

C. R. Simeon says, "There are three crowns: the crown of Torah, the crown of priesthood, and the crown of sovereignty.

D. "But the crown of a good name is best of them all" [M. 4:13].

A. R. Nehorai says, "Go into exile to a place of Torah, and do not suppose that it will come to you.

B. "For your fellow-disciples will make it solid in your hand.

C. "And on your own understanding do not rely" [M. 4:14].

4:15–22

A. R. Yannai says, "We do not have in hand [an explanation] either for the prosperity of the wicked or for the suffering of the righteous."

B. R. Matya b. Harash says, "Greet everybody first.

C. "And be a tail to lions,

D. "but do not be a head of foxes" [M. 4:15].

A. R. Jacob says, "This world is like an antechamber before the world to come.

B. "Get ready in the antechamber, so you can go into the great hall" [M. 4:16].

A. He would say, "Better is a single moment spent in penitence and good deeds in this world than the whole of the world to come.

B. "And better is a single moment of inner peace in the world to come than the whole of a lifetime spent in this world" [M. 4:17].

A. R. Simeon b. Eleazar says, "(1) Do not try to make amends to your fellow when he is angry,

B. "or (2) comfort him when the corpse of his [beloved] is lying before him,

C. "or (3) seek to find absolution for him at the moment at which he takes a vow,

D. "or (4) attempt to see him when he is humiliated" [M. 4:18].

A. Samuel the Small says, "*Rejoice not when your enemy falls, and let not your heart be glad when he is overthrown, lest the Lord see it and it displease him, and he turn away his wrath from him* (Prov. 24:17)" [M. 4:19].

A. Elisha b. Abuyah says, "He who learns when a child—what is he like? Ink put down on a clean piece of paper.

B. "And he who learns when an old man—what is he like? Ink put down on a paper full of erasures."

C. R. Yose b. R. Judah of Kefar Habbabli says, "He who learns from children—what is he like? One who eats sour grapes and drinks fresh wine.

D. "And he who learns from old men—what is he like? He who eats ripe grapes and drinks vintage wine."

E. Rabbi says, "Do not look at the bottle but at what is in it.

F. "You can have a new bottle full of old wine, and an old bottle which does not contain even new wine" [M. 4:20].

A. R. Eliezer Haqqappar says, "Jealousy, lust, and ambition drive a person out of this world" [M. 4:21].

A. He would say, "Those who are born are [destined] to die, and those who die are [destined] for resurrection.

B. "And the living are [destined] to be judged—

C. "so as to know, to make known, and to confirm that (1) he is God,

D. "(2) he is the one who forms,

E. "(3) he is the one who creates,

F. "(4) he is the one who understands,

G. "(5) he is the one who judges,

H. "(6) he is the one who gives evidence,

I. "(7) he is the one who brings suit,

J. "(8) and he is the one who is going to make the ultimate judgment.

K. "Blessed be he, for before him are not (1) guile, (2) forgetfulness, (3) respect for persons, (4) bribe-taking,

L. "for everything is his.

M. "And know that everything is subject to reckoning.

N. "And do not let your evil impulse persuade you that Sheol is a place of refuge for you.

O. "For (1) despite your wishes were you formed, (2) despite your wishes were you born, (3) despite your wishes do you live, (4) despite your wishes do you die, and (5) despite your wishes are you going to give a full accounting before the King of kings of kings, the Holy One blessed be he" [M. 4:22].

There seems to be a tendency to group sayings in units of two or four stichs, as indicated. Samuel the Small, M. 4:19, is given a scriptural verse as his saying. Eliezer's materials, M. 4:21–22, are out of all proportion to the rest. They also mark a note of finality, e.g., the barrage at M. 4:22K–O.

THE TORAH AS A PARTICULAR THING

The authors of Abot scarcely use the word Torah to refer to a particular thing or object, that is, a Torah-scroll. To be sure, we notice a number of points at which a verse of Scripture is cited. Accordingly, the notion that the Torah constitutes a particular body of authoritative writing certainly is present. But when the authors of this tractate refer to either "the Torah" or "Torah," they generally have in mind a less concrete sense of the word—learning, something that sages do. There is only one exceptional passage. The reference to "the essentials of the Torah" at M. Abot 3:18 presupposes that we deal with a particular book.

THE TORAH AS REVELATION

Before surveying the relevant passages, let us rapidly provide an overview of the available meanings. First, Torah means revelation, things God has said to Israel. Second, revelation is not necessarily only in writing. Third, and most important, when people study revelation, they enter into immediate relationship with God. So revelation in a book promises the possibility of the experience of revelation to those who study that book. Let us see these allegations in their settings.

The starting point is M. 1:1A: "Moses received Torah at Sinai." The contents of this Torah are not indicated. The context, however, precludes assuming that at issue is *only* the Torah contained in a Torah-scroll, that is, the written Torah. The contrary seems to be the meaning imputed in context. Revelation at Sinai then encompasses what the sages in the chain say.

"Making a fence for the Torah" (M. 1:1C3; 3:13B) and the reference of Simeon (M. 1:2B1) fall into the general category of revelation. "Drawing people near to the Torah" (M. Abot 1:12B) surely means to encourage people to live by revelation. I take it that all sayings on how studying Torah brings God's presence to the disciple, e.g., M. Abot 3:2–3, bear the clear implication that Torah is God's word. I see the same meaning at M. 3:6. But in these passages "revelation" takes on an active, immediate sense. "Studying revelation" produces an encounter with God('s presence). The Torah as revelation, in which we learn "how the world was made," occurs at M. 3:14G–I. The Torah (whatever its contents) then is a concrete scroll presenting God's revelation to Moses.

M. 3:11A5, interpreting the Torah improperly, need not demand the meaning "the written Torah," or "a particular document."

TORAH AS A PARTICULAR ACT.
AS GENERIC

Explicit allusions to "studying Torah" occur at M. Abot 1:5B; 1:15A ("make Torah a fixed obligation"). "Learning Torah" is contrasted with having an occupation, on the one side (M. Abot 2:2), or with carrying out religious duties enjoined in the Torah (M. Abot 3:5; 3:17) on the other. Both contrasts presuppose that study is what one does with Torah. "Torah" runs parallel to "life" (M. Abot 2:7B). Whether the reference is to studying Torah as prolonging life can hardly be settled in that context. However, M. 2:8B and 3:7 surely decide the matter: a person is created to "make his Torah great," and that surely means to learn much of what is in the Torah. This prolongs life, so 3:7. None of the disciples' sayings carries this motif forward. M. Abot 2:12 refers to making oneself ready to "learn Torah." Further statements on Torah-study as a particular act—what one does with The Torah and how one thereby becomes a sage and holy—are at M. Abot 2:14A; 2:16B; 3:2; 3:3; 3:11B as noted. M. Abot 3:7, 8 clearly state that studying Torah keeps a person alive, and ceasing to do so will kill him. Learning so as to teach and to do (M. Abot 4:5) defines the entire range of "Torah" as a particular act. "Labor in Torah" (M. Abot 4:10) can only mean "studying the Torah." "Meticulous study" (M. Abot 4:13) falls into the same classification. The reference to "a place of Torah" (M. Abot 4:14) is startling, since the meaning enlarges on the notion of a particular act. Now we speak even of a place in which people do that act. I see no passage in which *torah* stands generically, either for learning in general or for a general rule.

TORAH AS INDICATOR OF STATUS

The concrete allusions of the remaining sixty-two tractates of the Mishnah, reviewed above, find no parallel in Abot. Honoring the Torah and so being honored (M. Abot 4:6) makes explicit the relationship between "Torah" and personal status. M. Abot 4:9–10 promise concrete rewards. But we do not find the contrasting sense in which Torah stands for one status as against the lesser authority accruing to teachings from another document. For example, we find no citation attributed to a sage called "words of sages" in contrast with a citation of Scripture called "words of Torah." Proof-texts are just that; they do not establish a contrast between the status of two distinct but related sayings. This seems ample proof that the contrasting distinction of Torah as against scribes' sayings plays no role here. So status in the Mishnah's principal sense is not attested.

A Torah-person, a sage, of course, is everywhere at hand, and it is Torah that confers that status.

WRITTEN AND ORAL TORAH

Abot does not know this distinction in its mythic formulation.

TORAH AS A WAY OF LIFE

At M. Abot 3:5, Torah connotes not what one learns in particular, but a discipline in general. There, "the yoke of Torah" may mean "the work of persistently studying revelation." In any event, the line between a life of systematically memorizing Torah-sayings, on the one side, and a life expressive of Torah in the sense used in the story of a disciple hiding under a master's bed is not always clearly marked. One both studies and works to make a living; study of Torah is not advanced as the encompassing pattern of everyday life.

Time and again we shall find it difficult to classify a saying. References to a pattern of behavior in general may encompass every detail of life, but they may speak merely to the narrower acts of ritual learning. I am not inclined to see, in what we have reviewed, clear evidence that the word Torah alludes to anything more than the intellectual side of things—that is, things worth knowing.

TORAH AS A SOURCE OF SALVATION

So far as an individual wishes through the Torah to save himself from death and for life eternal, Abot may suggest, but does not make explicit, that salvation comes through the Torah. The rewards of Torah-study—curiously omitted in chapters 1 and 2—appear in sayings assigned to second-century figures. In the mouths of earlier sages, the issues are righteousness and justice, not Torah-study in particular; the sayings of chapters 1 and 2 do not promise salvation. When we are told that if an individual sits and labors at Torah, he receives a reward, and that if several people do so, God joins them at the task, then we still cannot confidently claim that study of the Torah produces salvation for either individual or community. In this life, Nehunia maintains (M. 3:5) that study of the Torah in a disciplined way frees one from the yoke of the state and of hard labor. But that and similar statements do not compare to those to be reviewed in the Talmuds that explicitly promise personal and national salvation through the Torah. So, in all, we must recognize the simple fact that Abot does not focus upon the study of Torah and the rewards for doing so, here or in the world to come.

TORAH AND SAGACITY

Abot draws into the orbit of Torah-talk the names of authorities of the Mishnah. But we now see clearly that Abot does not claim that the Mishnah forms part of the Torah. Nor, obviously, does the tractate we have reviewed know the doctrine of the two Torahs. Only in the Talmuds do we begin to find clear and ample evidence of that doctrine. Abot, moreover, does not understand by the word Torah much more than the framers of the Mishnah do. Not only does the established classification scheme remain intact, but the sense of the items we have surveyed essentially replicates already familiar usages, producing no innovation. On the contrary, I find a diminution in the range of meanings.

Yet Abot in the aggregate *does* differ from the Mishnah. The difference has to do with the topic at hand. The other sixty-two tractates of the Mishnah contain Torah-sayings here and there. But they do not fall within the framework of Torah-discourse. They speak about other matters entirely. The consideration of the status of Torah rarely pertains to that speech. Abot, by contrast, says a great deal about Torah-study. The claim that Torah-study produces direct encounter with God forms part of Abot's thesis about the Torah. That claim, by itself, will hardly have surprised Israelite writers of wisdom books over a span of many centuries, whether those assembled in the Essene commune at Qumran, on the one side, or those represented in the pages of Proverbs and in many of the Psalms, or even the Deuteronomistic circle, on the other.

A second glance at our tractate, however, produces a surprising fact. In Abot, Torah is instrumental. The figure of the sage, his ideals and conduct, forms the goal, focus and center. To state matters simply: Abot regards study of Torah as what a sage does. The substance of Torah is what a sage says. That is so whether or not the saying relates to scriptural revelation. The content of the sayings attributed to sages endows those sayings with self-validating status. The sages usually do not quote verses of Scripture and explain them, nor do they speak in God's name. Yet, it is clear, sages talk Torah. What follows? It is this: if a sage says something, what he says is Torah. More accurately, what he says falls into the classification of Torah. Accordingly, as I said, Abot treats Torah-learning as symptomatic, an indicator of the status of the sage, hence, as I said, as merely instrumental.

The simplest proof of that proposition lies in the recurrent formal structure of the document, the one thing the framers of the document never omit and always emphasize: (1) the *name* of the authority behind a saying, from Simeon the Righteous on downward, and (2) the connective-attributive *"says."* So what is important to the redactors is what they never have to tell us. Because a recognized sage makes a statement, what he says constitutes, in and of itself, a statement in the status of Torah.

To spell out what this means, let us look back at the opening sentences. Moses received Torah, and it reached the Men of the Great Assembly. The three things those men said bear no resemblance to anything we find in written Scripture. They focus upon the life of sagacity—prudence, discipleship, a fence around the Torah. And, as we proceed, we find time and again that, while the word Torah stands for two things, divine revelation and the act of study of divine revelation, it produces a single effect, the transformation of unformed man into sage. One climax comes in Yohanan ben Zakkai's assertion that the purpose for which a man (an Israelite) was created was to study Torah, followed by his disciples' specifications of the most important things to be learned in the Torah. All of these pertain to the conduct of the wise man, the sage.

When we review the classifications among which we earlier divided references to Torah in Abot, we find our catalogues merely perfunctory. In fact, in those taxa we miss the most important points of emphasis of the tractate. That is why, as I said, we have to locate the document's focus not on Torah but on the life of sagacity (including, to be sure, Torah-study). But what defines and delimits Torah? It is the sage himself. So we may simply state the tractate's definition of Torah: Torah is what a sage learns. Accordingly, the Mishnah contains

Torah. It may well be thought to fall into the classification of Torah. But the reason, we recognize, is that authorities whose sayings are found in the Mishnah possess Torah from Sinai. What they say, we cannot overemphasize, is Torah. How do we know it? *It is a fact validated by the association of what they say with their own names.*

So we miss the real issue when we ask Abot to explain for us the status of the Mishnah, or to provide a theory of a dual Torah. The principal point of insistence—the generative question—before the framers of Abot does not address the status of the Mishnah. And the instrumental status of the Torah, as well as of the Mishnah, lies in the net effect of their composition: the claim that through study of the Torah sages enter God's presence. So study of Torah serves a further goal, that of forming sages. The theory of Abot pertains to the religious standing and consequence of the learning of the sages. To be sure, a secondary effect of that theory endows with the status of revealed truth things sages say. But then, as I have stressed, it is because they say them, not because they have heard them in an endless chain back to Sinai. The fundament of truth is passed on through sagacity, not through already formulated and carefully memorized truths. That is why the single most important word in Abot also is the most common, the word *"says."*

To summarize: At issue in Abot is not Torah, but the authority of the sage. It is that standing that transforms a saying into a Torah-saying, or to state matters more appropriately, that places a saying into the classification of Torah. Abot then stands as the first document of incipient rabbinism, that is, of the doctrine that the sage embodies the Torah and is a holy man, like Moses "our rabbi," in the likeness and image of God. The beginning is to claim that a saying falls into the category of Torah if a sage says it as Torah. The end will be to view the sage himself as Torah incarnate.

3

Tosefta:
Torah in the Mishnah's
First Talmud

THE MISHNAH'S FIRST TALMUD

The Tosefta provides a large corpus of rules formulated in the same syntax and structure as those of the Mishnah, which in fact they supplement. The compilation as a whole runs roughly four times the Mishnah in size. The Tosefta's supplements to the Mishnah's statements fall into three categories. First, the Tosefta may cite a statement in the Mishnah verbatim and amplify it in some way. That first type of passage comes closest to what the two Talmuds later on would provide as Mishnah-exegesis. Second, the Tosefta's passage may be framed as an autonomous statement, yet can be fully understood only in relationship to its Mishnaic counterpart. In the third type, the Tosefta's rule stands entirely independent of any specific formulation in the Mishnah's corresponding passage, though in theme or principle the Tosefta's statement may bear a close relationship to the Mishnah's formulation. The first two classifications encompass the vast majority of statements in the Tosefta. Only the third type of statement may be thought to originate in the time in which the authors of the Mishnah were doing their work. The first and second types must be post-Mishnaic.

The document as a whole seems to have taken shape in the two hundred years beyond the closure of the Mishnah. All named authorities cited in the Tosefta, however, are assumed to have flourished in the period in which the Mishnah was written, the first and second centuries. They normally bear the same names as Mishnaic sages. So in its repertoire of usable names, imitation of Mishnaic style and syntax, and dependence upon the Mishnah's redactional structure, the

Tosefta may be compared to a work of pseudepigrapha. For though the Tosefta pretends to be a second Mishnah, in fact it serves simply as a sort of Talmud—that is, a compendious and systematic exegesis of the Mishnah.

THE TORAH AS A PARTICULAR THING

The Torah as a scroll of revelation is something one may not burn (T. Shab. 14:4), make into a pile (T. Meg. 4:20), bind with cloths set aside for that purpose (T. Meg. 4:20). The Torah-scroll in particular occurs at T. Ter. 1:10; T. B.B. 8:14; T. Er. 8:6; T. Sot. 7:18; 15:3; T. B.Q. 11:3; T. B.M. 3:24; 11:23 (Torah-scroll as distinct from a scroll containing the Prophets); T. San. 4:7; T. Par. 10:8; T. Ah. 14:6. An oath taken by "this Torah" occurs at T. Pe. 3:2. "The Torah" as a set of written passages is mentioned at T. Meg. 4:18; T. Sot. 8:7. "Reading in the Torah" understood as a concrete text appears at T. Ber. 2:12, now matched against "repeating Mishnah-traditions." When, at T. Suk. 2:10, we find a tale of Israelites carrying a Torah wherever they go, the reference can be only to a physical object. "Beginning with the Torah" (T. R.H. 4:6) refers to reading a passage in the Torah. One sells his Torah, meaning a Torah-scroll (T. B.Q. 2:15). The king writes two Torahs, one to keep at home and one for when he travels (T. San. 4:8)—assuredly a physical object.

THE TORAH AS REVELATION

"That which is written in the Torah of your servant, Moses" (T. Yoma 2:1) provides the best example of the present category: the *contents* of the Torah-scroll. The "giving of the Torah" occurs at T. San. 4:7. ("Ezra was worthy that Torah should have been given through him.") The "giving of the Torah," meaning the time of revelation at Sinai, is at T. Hul. 7:8 and T. Par. 4:8.

"Torah" meaning something precious, but not necessarily a particular object, occurs at T. Hor. 2:7. "The Torah is made up of one theme or topic after another" (T. San. 7:7), and that surely means that the Torah is a composition of diverse materials.

Torah refers to revelation in general, not to a particular object but to the contents thereof, also at T. Ber. 7:23, "At first, when Torah was common[ly known] in Israel. . . ." The meaning would be "knowledge" of Torah. (Whether the reference is to written or oral Torah is not settled.) Torah is studied ("When I was studying Torah") at T. Er. 8:6; T. Suk. 2:3; T. Ed. 2:2; and so on. "The Torah" also encompasses dimensions of interpretation ("chambers . . . ") (T. Ket. 5:11; T. San. 12:9). A student masters Torah-learning in an organized sequence of steps. I see the same sense at T. Er. 11:24; T. Hag. 1:9. "Torah" is something one teaches his son, parallel to teaching him the *Shema* or the Hebrew language, at T. Hag. 1:2. "Torah" is something that remains with the son and so is remembered. "The Torah," encompassing all rules, is at T. Shab. 9:6. "A blessing said over the Torah," meaning not the object but the whole corpus of divine revelation, occurs at T. Yoma 4:18; T. B.M. 6:17. Torah-passages heard in synagogue worship are noted at T. R.H. 4:6.

"Torah" furthermore stands for a particular body of revealed law in statements such as this: "Torah has said" followed by a factual allegation or a rule. That sort of statement is not necessarily followed by an explicit citation of Scripture. We find, rather, allusions to established facts enjoying the status of Torah-law, as much as to actual verses. In the former category are the following passages: T. Ber. 7:19; T. Pe. 1:6; T. Ter. 6:4 ("Torah has imposed a more stringent rule . . . "); T. Shab. 16:16; T. Suk. 3:18; T. Meg. 4:24; T. Ket. 13:3; T. Git. 9:4; T. B.Q. 3:3; 6:4; 7:2; T. San. 6:6; 8:3; T. Mak. 4:17 ("The scourging [decreed by the law of the] Torah [involves forty (stripes) less one"]; T. Men. 5:6; T. Bekh. 6:11; T. Ar. 2:10, 19. The "principal points of the Torah" occurs at T. Shab. 2:10. "Teachings of Torah" (T. Dem. 2:4, 5) refers to the principles of Judaism. The same phrase at T. Sot. 7:11 signifies teachings of the Torah in a less specific sense, so too at T. B.Q. 7:13; T. Hal. 2:24; T. Sot. 8:7; T. San. 14:13. The Torah as a source of defined measurements is at T. B.M. 2:4, or other established facts. In the latter category in which we find Torah as revealed Scripture, cited verbatim, are these references: T. Sot. 7:20, "Torah has taught . . . " followed by proof-texts for the stated proposition and T. San. 4:7. More common is the claim that a given view derives from "the Torah," followed by citation of a verse of Scripture. Such instances are as follows: T. Ber. 6:1; 7:2; T. Ter. 1:10; T. B.B. 8:14; and T. Sot. 5:13.

References to "what is stated," or "written," in the Torah, not joined to a cited verse of Scripture, are found at T. Kil. 1:9; T. Bik. 2:4, 5; T. Shab. 1:7; 11:19; T. Meg. 4:5, 17, 18, 20. T. Hag. 1:3 refers to "all the religious requirements that are stated in the Torah." Further allusions to "that which appears or is written in the Torah" occur as follows: T. Qid. 3:7, 8; 9:2; T. Naz. 2:2; T. Git. 9:1, 2; T. Ned. 1:4; T. Sot. 7:4; T. Shebu. 2:15, 16; T. Hor. 1:7 ("in the Torah" meaning, among statements or rules found therein); T. Hul. 10:16, 18; T. Ar. 1:5; T. Ker. 1:18; T. Neg. 8:2; T. Par. 1:5, 6; T. Toh. 2:1. "The Torah has assigned to them" refers to a rule found in the Torah. Religious duties or facts specified "in the Torah" further appear at T. Pe. 3:8; 4:19; T. Shab. 9:3; 14:4; T. Yad. 2:12; T. Pes. 6:3, 4; T. Sheq. 3:21; T. Ker. 1:12; T. Ned. 2:6; T. Sot. 1:10; 7:2, 3; 8:11; T. Git. 9:1; T. B.M. 8:22, 23, 24; T. Shebu. 6:1; T. San. 10:11; 13:6; T. Mak. 1:11; 5:16; T. Shebu. 1:3, 5; 3:7; 6:1; T. A.Z. 4:3; T. Men. 12:9; T. Bes. 3:11, 12; T. Me. 1:13; T. Ker. 1:6, 16; T. Toh. 1:3.

TORAH AS A PARTICULAR ACT.
AS GENERIC

"Studying" or "teaching Torah" as a performed action occurs at T. Er. 8:6; T. Ket. 4:6; T. Sot. 8:6; 15:10; T. Qid. 1:11; 5:16 (also "Torah" meaning the action, without the verb, at T. Qid. 5:16); T. B.M. 3:25; T. B.B. 10:4; T. A.Z. 1:8 = T. M.Q. 2:1; T. Bekh. 6:10; T. Ah. 16:8 = T. Par. 4:7. Explicit reference to the act of "study of Torah" appears at T. Pe. 1:1; T. M.Q. 2:1; T. A.Z. 1:5; 2:6. "When Israelites are engaged in the Torah" (T. Suk. 2:10) surely refers to the time of their studying, rather than, for instance, to acts of labor with a material object. Bringing a son "to the Torah" (T. Ber. 7:12) means to introduce him to (the act of studying) the Torah.

Torah bearing a generic meaning, e.g., "torah" as a definitive rule, occurs at T. Zeb. 10:9, complementing the counterpart passage at M. The generic sense of *torah* as "the rule governing . . . " also is used at T. Er. 9:6. "Torah" in the clear meaning of a taxon or classification appears at T. Kel. B.Q. 6:12: "not in the category (Torah) of utensils."

TORAH AS INDICATOR OF STATUS

When the framers of the Tosefta refer to "the Torah has said" plus a rule or norm, they ordinarily mean that that rule or norm enjoys the status of "Torah," hence the highest authority. The references have already been catalogued above. The notion of a teaching or rule deriving from the higher authority of the Torah, in contradiction to the lesser authority of scribes, does occur. The appearances are as follows: T. Ta. 2:6; T. Yeb. 2:4; T. Qid. 5:21; T. T.Y. 1:10; T. Ed. 1:1, 5 ("one imposes a strict ruling in the case of a rule deriving from the Torah, a lenient one in the case of a law given by scribes"); T. Par. 11:5; T. Ter. 1:10; T. B.B. 8:14 ("defined by the Torah"); T. Yeb. 6:4, 7 ("Torah laid down . . . sages ruled . . ."); T. Sot. 5:13; T. B.M. 2:28; 8:9; T. Shebu. 1:7; T. Zeb. 13:15; T. Men. 10:26; 11:5; T. Tem. 1:17; T. Ar. 3:6; T. Ker. 1:17 (in all, a detail prescribed by the Torah in particular); T. Miq. 5:4; T. Zab. 5:1.

"Sons of Torah" (T. B.Q. 7:6,7) serve as "atonement for the world." They therefore enjoy a particular supernatural status. Knowledge of "Torah" gives the son higher status than the father (T. Bekh. 6:10). The Tosefta's supplement to M. Sot. 9:15 "honor of the Torah" presents "the arms of the Torah" (T. Sot. 16:3), as well as "the honor . . ." (T. Sot. 14:3, 8). All of these usages are familiar from the Mishnah. None represents a secondary development.

WRITTEN AND ORAL TORAH

The counterpart of Scripture is Mishnah (T. Ber. 2:12). But that usage does not demand reference to the mythic language to encompass both within the Torah. The framers of the Tosefta never refer to the myth of the dual Torah, nor do they know the Mishnah in particular as either Torah or oral Torah.

TORAH AS A WAY OF LIFE

It is not always easy to distinguish use of the word Torah to mean a life of studying the Torah, on the one side, from use of the same word to encompass the entire holy way of life decreed by the Torah as sages taught it, on the other. This much broader usage makes the word Torah connote the entire system we should call "Judaism." The criterion for recognizing the latter intent, as distinct from the former, is as follows. If in context we discern that the word Torah stands for something more than a book or corpus of revelation mastered by a disciple, and if, further, Torah refers to the supernatural standing of the entire people of Israel, then "Torah" connotes the holy way of life we should now name Judaism.

When the Tosefta's framers speak of "studying Torah" or "teaching Torah," however, they refer to a pattern of learning that transforms the disciple and the master, not merely imparts information. Accordingly, every point listed in the section Torah as Indicator of Status attests to this larger construction of the word Torah. Evidence of the broader meaning is at T. Qid. 5:16 and T. B.M. 2:30, where "Torah" is contrasted with a craft or way of making a living, and T. B.M. 3:25, where personal traits constitute a criterion for the acceptability of a disciple who wishes to study Torah. "How can X, who has done such-and-so, now present himself to study Torah?" "A disciple who abandoned the Torah" (T. Hag. 1:8) is one who has apostasized, so too at T. San. 13:5. "Taking a vow against 'the Torah'" (T. Ned. 1:4) surely alludes to the way of life as a whole, rather than some specific doctrine alone. So too Abraham's keeping "the Torah" (T. Qid. 5:21) refers to the whole way of life, "all that is written therein." "The righteous love the Torah" (T. Zeb. 2:17) refers not to the object or the contents in particular, but to something more abstract that transcends both. So too "if one has forgotten the Torah" (T. Ker. 2:9), he has forgotten the entire thing, all at once, and not merely a particular teaching. When we find a statement such as, "My soul yearns for Torah" (T. Yeb. 8:4), the sense is deeper and richer than a desire merely for learning. The usage "labor in the Torah" (T. Men. 13:22) usually bears a narrower meaning of Torah-learning. As to "when you see that the Torah is esteemed by Israelites" (T. Ber. 7:24), the meaning seems broader than either the act of learning or knowledge in general. Rather, the connotation encompasses the entire Torah-enterprise. I see the same broad sense at T. Ber. 7:24, "They have nullified your Torah—it is time to work for the Lord."

Finally, dissension in "the Torah" yielded "two Torahs," meaning "two camps" or parties (T. Sot. 14:9). This usage is the most figurative of all. Yet it is in no way generic. "Torah" retains its specificity as the right, revealed doctrine. But the connotative meaning, I think, places the entry into the present classification.

TORAH AS A SOURCE OF SALVATION

The framers of the Tosefta stay as close as they possibly can to the style and sense of the Mishnah. Accordingly, in the Tosefta it is difficult to find a doctrine that the Mishnah omits, or to miss one that the Mishnah emphasizes. It follows that our discussion of the salvific value of the Torah in the Mishnah applies without variation to what we find, and do not find, in the Tosefta. This fact is surprising when we consider that the Tosefta took shape in the same two centuries in which the two Talmuds came into being. We can come to only one conclusion: the people who worked on the Tosefta followed one set of conventions, while those sages (the same or others) who worked on the units of discourse ultimately gathered into the two Talmuds followed a different set.

We therefore cannot differentiate layers in the history of ideas by appealing to the sequence in which several documents are assumed successively to have come to closure. If Abot and the Tosefta were composed in the later third and fourth centuries, respectively, then, as I said, they emerge from pretty much the same hands that at about the same time were writing down the units of discourse we now find in the two Talmuds and parts of the compositions of exegesis (midrashim) as well. For the Talmuds, the word Torah carries the sense of salvation, in both concrete and abstract ways, while for the documents at hand—those closest in style and redaction to the Mishnah—the word Torah bears no such sense.

What we survey turns out to be conventions and preferences of editors, not the prevailing public usage of the word or the conceptions implicit in it. So when we find that the word Torah appears in the Tosefta to bear no salvific implications whatsoever, that fact testifies to the character of the Tosefta, not to the diminishing or expanding meanings generally assigned to the word Torah in public discourse among sages. True, the movement from scroll to symbol begins in the Mishnah and ends in the Talmuds. But that is a literary, not a temporal and historical, progression.

THE TOSEFTA'S THEORY
OF THE TORAH

The Tosefta supplements the Mishnah but, for the topic at hand, in no way moves beyond the limits of discourse defined by the Mishnah. Whatever we find in the Mishnah appears also in the Tosefta, and whatever meanings or nuances the Mishnah fails to explore, the Tosefta likewise ignores. The stunning innovation represented by the thesis of tractate Abot, that the sage confers the status of Torah upon a saying, makes no impact at all upon the formulation of the word Torah in the Tosefta.

4

The Talmud of the
Land of Israel

The Talmud of the Land of Israel, generally believed to have reached closure about 400 C.E., provides a systematic exegesis of thirty-nine of the Mishnah's sixty-two tractates, in particular, for the first four of the Mishnah's six divisions: Agriculture, Appointed Times, Women, and Damages. It omits reference to all of Holy Things, and, in Purities, treats only a few chapters of Niddah. For the tractates it takes up, it does two things. First, this Talmud provides a line-by-line exegesis of small sense- or thought-units of the Mishnah, treated discretely, a few lines at a time, very often doing the same for corresponding units of the Tosefta. Second, the Talmud undertakes a more wide-ranging discourse about larger problems of biblical exegesis, theology, and principles of law. Accordingly, the Talmud presents both exegesis of its organizing text, the Mishnah, and systematic expansion and exposition of ideas or principles abstracted from, and covering several discrete units of, the base text. Of the whole, I estimate that approximately ninety percent in volume consists of the first kind, ten percent the second kind of discourse.

Testimony to the remarkably fresh and independent attitude of mind in the Talmud of the Land of Israel emerges from its contrast to both Abot and Tosefta. Both of these look back upon the Mishnah, remaining closely tied to the Mishnah both in rhetoric and in forms and modes of discourse. The Tosefta augments and expands the Mishnah (while Abot accounts for the standing of its authorities) without ever really leaving the framework of the Mishnah itself. That framework, whether in the organization and redaction of ideas, or in the modes of formulation and conception, dictates the literary character and exegetical agenda of the Tosefta, a vine hanging from the Mishnah's trellis.

The Talmud of the Land of Israel, by contrast, steps back from the Mishnah. The authors pick up its individual sentences, work over and rework them one by one in accordance with the Talmud's own program of inquiry. They construct problems for investigation entirely separate from the issues of a given, limited passage of the Mishnah itself.

The Talmud, moreover, completely ignores the rhetoric and language of the Mishnah. It is composed not in Mishnaic Hebrew but, for passages in which the Talmud's framers speak with their own voice, in a kind of scholastic rhetoric, of Aramaic. Its exercises of comparison and contrast of passages of Mishnah and of Tosefta define for the Talmud a stance and a platform of its own. The Talmud's composers stand back from both documents and weigh and measure passages of each in a balance of their own construction.

Again, the authors of the Talmud of the Land of Israel not only pick and choose for extended analysis passages of the Mishnah and the Tosefta. They also decide which entire tractates to endow with a Talmud, and which ones simply to ignore—with amazing selectivity and astonishing independence of judgment. Since we have Tosefta-tractates for nearly all Mishnah-tractates, the contrast is clear. In these three ways and in many others the Talmud of the Land of Israel opens new paths in the exploration of the Torah, plumbs unimagined depths of meaning in what lay at hand.

Since for the Talmud of the Land of Israel we have no concordance extending beyond *Alef*, we cannot undertake a thorough survey of the established meanings of the word Torah. But that fact makes no difference at all. For the Talmud of the Land of Israel rests upon the foundations of the Mishnah, on the one side, and draws vast quantities of materials from the Tosefta, on the other. Consequently, we may simply stipulate at the outset that the familiar meanings of the word occur in abundance. It will suffice to give a few instances of how, in the Yerushalmi, people use the word Torah in familiar and established ways. Only at the end shall we turn to what I believe to be an essentially fresh usage of the word, a sense for which, so far as I can discern, we know no precedent in documents surveyed to date.

Examination of the Talmud of the Land of Israel for the present survey covers the following tractates in my translation (or in that of my colleagues): Berakhot (Zahavy), Terumot (Avery-Peck), Maaserot (Jaffee), Maaser Sheni (Haas), Hallah, Orlah, Bikkurim, Shabbat, Erubin, Yoma, Sheqalim, Rosh Hashanah (Goldman), Sukkah, Besah, Taanit, Megillah, Hagigah, Moed Qatan, Yebamot, Ketubot, Nedarim, Nazir, Gittin, Qiddushin, Sotah, Baba Qamma, Baba Mesia, Baba Batra, Sanhedrin, Makkot, Shebuot, Abodah Zarah, Horayot, and Niddah. Omitted are Peah, Demai, Kilayim, Shebiit, and Pesahim, because they are not yet available for ready reference in English.

Before turning to this survey, we must take note of the single most striking conception exhibited in this Talmud, a conception that no survey of references to the word Torah will reveal. It is that, in the Talmud of the Land of Israel, our sages treat the Mishnah precisely as they do the written Torah. They subject both to exactly the same methods of exegesis, for one thing. They cite both and explain, in pretty much the same modes of thought, the meanings they find. This equivalence of Mishnah and Scripture, moreover, emerges not only in implicit, but also in explicit ways. We find sayings that weigh the merit of studying the Torah against the merit of studying the Mishnah—something without parallel in the documents surveyed above. Alongside, in these same sayings, discourse takes up such other categories as laws (halakhot).

Accordingly, we enter the document with an awareness that the fundamental stability of the pattern of familiar meanings now imputed to the word Torah in this composition obscures a deeper shift. Other classifications of statements, other completed documents, weigh in the balance against the Torah-statement and the written Torah. Whether or not we speculate that people reached the conclusion that, since the Mishnah enjoyed the status of the (written) Torah, therefore the Mishnah constituted part of the (one whole) Torah revealed to Moses (our rabbi) makes no difference. The implicit advance toward that ultimate conception moves in its own path, step by step. The most subtle, yet most consequential, step is the first one, How so? Once something is perceived as *like* the Torah, or at the level of the Torah, things ultimately will move in the direction in which we know they ultimately did. What is like the Torah enters the status of, and ultimately becomes, Torah.

So what does not appear in the plethora of examples of familiar usages not cited in detail, or in the few examples we now take up, is the incipient sense that the Mishnah—and therefore much else—must find a location in relationship to Scripture. This emerging consciousness of the Mishnah as a completed document, demanding a place in the larger theory of revelation, constitutes the single stunning contribution of the Talmud of the Land of Israel. This is, in the last analysis, a protracted commentary on the Mishnah. The problem presented by the need to frame a theory of the Mishnah (as distinct from systematic exegesis of discrete passages of the Mishnah) in the Talmud produces the first evidence of a dramatic shift of meanings imputed to the word Torah.

In what way? Let me summarize my argument. First comes the comparison of X (standing for the Mishnah) to Y (standing for Scripture), that is, the issue of how X relates to Y. Then emerges the conviction that X *is* Y, Mishnah is Torah. But, as we shall see, the Talmud at hand presents a still more surprising fact: it defines a new taxon altogether, that is, a fresh category for classification.

THE TORAH AS A PARTICULAR THING

We recognize, of course, the cumulative character of the canon. The Torah occurs as an object—a Torah-scroll: at Y. San. 2:6.III, the king writes his own Torah-scroll. In the present instance, both Mishnah and Tosefta stand behind the Talmud's usage. The Samaritans forged their own Torah (Y. Sot. 7:37)—hence, a particular document. Two examples of the Yerushalmi's usage follow:

> Y. Megillah 4:1:[II.A] What is the law as to standing before a scroll of the Torah?
> [B] R. Hilqiah, R. Simon in the name of R. Eleazar: "Before her child [a disciple of a sage], she stands up; is it not an argument *a fortiori* that one stands up before the Torah itself?"
> Y. Bikkurim 3:6:[N] When R. Hananiah came, R. Phineas, R. Yohanan in the name of Rabban Simeon b. Gamaliel: "A man may sell a scroll of the Torah to get funds to marry a wife or to study Torah, and all the more so to save his life [by buying food]."

It goes without saying that instances in which the Torah is a scroll could be duplicated many times over. But we should not miss the Talmud's striking assertion in the first of these two examples. Since we stand up before a sage, we must also stand up before a Torah-scroll. Accordingly, the sage, not the Torah "as such," stands at the center of the argument, just as we noticed in tractate Abot.

THE TORAH AS REVELATION

When we find passages containing scriptural proof-texts, these testify to the view that the Torah is revealed and presents the decisive truth about the issue at hand. Such passages occur very frequently in the Talmud of the Land of Israel, which is, after all, concerned to systematically provide proof-texts for the Mishnah's propositions. In the following cases (among thousands), the framers explicitly cite the Torah, *always* meaning a verse of Scripture. Here are several instances in which the Torah "says" or otherwise validates a proposition culled from a single tractate: Y. Hor. 1:1,6 ("it is written" plus a cited verse), 8; 2:4, 5, 7; 3:1 (a teaching of Torah), 2, 3, 4, 5. In fact, a second glance shows that every pericope of that tractate refers directly or indirectly to scriptural proof-texts of some sort. A catalogue similar to that given below, for the Talmud of Babylonia, would require much space to prove a simple point. Accordingly, we stipulate, without further ado, that the Talmud of the Land of Israel systematically and thoroughly provides scriptural proof-texts for the Mishnah's, the Tosefta's, and the sages' propositions, and in diverse other ways treats the Torah as the source of divine revelation. Whether a passage specifies "the Torah has said," or "in accord with that which is written [in Scripture]," or "as it is said," the implication for the conception of "Torah" is always the same. The Torah, God's revelation to Israel, encompasses Hebrew Scripture alone.

In the Talmud at hand, however, "a word of Torah" may encompass the Mishnah's contents as much as those of Scripture. That presents enormously suggestive evidence of a shift in the meaning of the word Torah. In the following passage, the status of "Torah" is given to the words of the Mishnah. How so? Mishnah's statement serves as a proof-text as much as does the cited verse of Scripture[!]:

Y. Sanhedrin 6:10:[III.A] R. Abbahu was bereaved. One of his children had passed away from him. R. Yohanan and R. Yose went up [to comfort him]. When they called on him, out of reverence for him, they did not utter to him a word of Torah. He said to them, "May the rabbis utter a word of Torah."

[B] They said to him, "Let our master teach us."

[C] He said to them, "Now if in regard to the [earthly] government below, in which there is no reliability, [but only] lying, deceit, favoritism, and bribe-taking—

[D] "which is here today and gone tomorrow—

[E] "if concerning that government, it is said, *And the relatives of the felon come and inquire after the welfare of the judges and of the witnesses, as if to say, 'We have nothing against you, for you judged honestly* (M. San. 6:10),'

[F] "in regard to the government above, in which there is reliability, no lying, deceit, favoritism, or bribe-taking—

[G] "and which endures forever and to all eternity—

[H] "all the more so are we obligated to accept upon ourselves the just decree [of that heavenly government]."

[I] And it says, *"That the Lord . . . may show you mercy, and have compassion on you . . ."* (Deut. 13:17).

The italicized words at E cite a passage of the Mishnah verbatim, while those at I use Scripture. Both provide proof of the same value, and, it follows, the Mishnah enjoys the status of Scripture and forms an equal part of the Torah. But in general, when the Talmud goes in search of proof-texts, it looks at revealed Scripture. That search for revelation testifies to a paramount—but no longer principal —meaning of the word Torah in the Talmud: revealed Scripture. To be sure, God may reveal his will through means not deemed Torah at all; an echo from heaven, for example (Y. Qid. 1:1), may declare the decided law. But the principal and authoritative source of revelation is Scripture.

TORAH AS A PARTICULAR ACT.
AS GENERIC

One may know "the entire Torah," meaning in context the written one alone, as at Y. Hor. 1:1. The master teaches Torah, citing and expounding a verse of Scripture (Y. Hor. 3:1). A house of study is a holy place because the Torah is studied in it (Y. Hor. 3:4). The act of study may be described by various metaphors. One striking instance follows:

Y. Sanhedrin 2:5:[IV.A] It is written, "And David said longingly, 'O that some one would give me water to drink from the well of Bethlehem [which is by the gate']" (1 Chron. 11:17).
[B] R. Hiyya bar Ba said, "He requested a teaching of law."
[C] "Then the three mighty men broke through [the camp of the Philistines]" (1 Chron. 11:18).
[D] Why three? Because the law is not decisively laid down by fewer than three.
[E] "But David would not drink of it; [he poured it out to the Lord, and said, 'Far be it from me before my God that I should do this. Shall I drink the lifeblood of these men? For at the risk of their lives they brought it']" (1 Chron. 11:18–19).
[F] David did not want the law to be laid down in his own name.
[G] "He poured it out to the Lord"—establishing [the decision] as [an unattributed] teaching for the generations [so that the law should be authoritative and so be cited anonymously].

In this passage, the act of Torah-study is read into a verse of Scripture that speaks of warfare. A "word of Torah" serves various purposes. It generally means a Torah-teaching.

Torah as generic occurs as well, but I find no example that in any way changes the sense established in the instances found in the Mishnah.

TORAH AS INDICATOR OF STATUS

The distinction between a law enjoying the status of Scripture (Torah) as against one having only the lesser status of a teaching of scribes occurs at Y. A.Z.2:7, "the words of scribes are more precious than the words of Torah" (so too Y. San. 11:4). In the following instance, the distinction between law as laid down in the Torah and law as laid down by scribes shows us how the exegetes invoked that distinction to explain away conflicting points of law:

Y. Sukkah 3:11:[I.A] It is written, "You shall rejoice before the Lord your God seven days" (Lev. 23:40).
[B] There is a Tanna who teaches, "It is of the rejoicing with the *lulab* that Scripture speaks."
[C] There is a Tanna who teaches, "It is of the rejoicing [brought on by eating the meat] of peace-offerings that the Scripture speaks."
[D] [The written text: He who has said that it is of the rejoicing of

peace-offerings that Scripture speaks maintains that rejoicing on the first day is based on the authority of the Torah, and doing so on the other days is on the authority of the Torah as well.] He who says that it is of the rejoicing with the *lulab* that Scripture speaks holds that rejoicing on the first day is based on the authority of the Torah, and doing so on the other days also is based on the authority of the Torah.

[E] Consequently, in making his ordinance [M. Suk. 3:11, transferring to the provinces the Temple rite of carrying the *lulab* all seven days, doing in the synagogue what was done in the Temple], R. Yohanan ben Zakkai made his ordinance in reliance upon the law of the Torah.

[F] But he who has said that it is of rejoicing with the *lulab* that the Scripture spoke for the first day, as a matter of Torah law, but for the other days it was as a matter of law based on the authority of scribes, holds that Rabban Yohanan ben Zakkai made his decree rest on the authority of scribes [as well]. [Now the carrying of the *lulab* all seven days in the Temple was an ordinance of scribes, and doing so in the provinces, after the destruction, was an ordinance based on the authority of scribes tacked on to an ordinance based on the authority of scribes.]

This distinction between teachings of the Torah and teachings of the scribes emerged, as we saw, from the Mishnah. It predictably will occur in the Yerushalmi wherever it appears in the Mishnah. When we come to the Talmud of Babylonia, we shall see that this distinction forms the single most powerful and ubiquitous exegetical tool of the authors of that document. But in the Talmud at hand, it is difficult to locate fresh or systematic utilization of the stated distinction for exegetical purposes. The Mishnah's usage of Torah in contradistinction to scribal teaching, therefore, remains, if well in evidence, essentially static in the Yerushalmi.

The use of the word Torah as a classification indicating elevated status of persons, places, or things becomes fully articulated in our Talmud. The principal reference is to persons, that is, people enjoying the status of the Torah, sages in particular.

Y. Sheqalim 5:1:[I.E] Said R. Eliezer, "It is written, 'This Ezra went up from Babylonia. He was a scribe skilled in the law of Moses which the Lord the God of Israel had given; and the king granted him all that he asked, for the hand of the Lord his God was upon him' (Ezra 7:6. Why does Scripture say, 'scribe'?

[F] "Just as he was a scribe for teachings of Torah, so he was a scribe for teachings of sages."

The master of Torah enjoys an independent position vis-à-vis the patriarch (Y. Hor. 3:1). How so? He instructs the patriarch in the Torah. When a master of Torah says a prayer, it is heard in heaven (Y. Hor. 3:4). People who honor sages will surely benefit. One gives precedence to his master over his father, the former enjoying a greater right of respect (Y. Hor. 3:4, 5). When a family attains merit through learning, it rises in formal status (Y. Hor. 3:5). An elder (sage) is of higher status than a prophet (Y. A.Z.2:7). When great sages die, the natural world takes note by exhibiting supernatural events (Y. A.Z.3:1). The sage enjoys a higher status than the patriarch (Y. A.Z.3:1). But the sage may well support himself through menial labor (Y. San. 2:6).

But these matters of social priority of the sage do not lead us to the heart of the matter. They reveal only the effects of a deeper conviction. The sage enjoys the high status accorded to him because he possesses and transmits Torah-sayings. That fact endows him with the status of the Torah—*and of the One who gave the Torah.* That claim to students of Judaism through the ages constitutes little more than a self-evident cliché. But in the literature that took shape before Yerushalmi, we do not find such a claim. And, as we are now coming to realize, the equation of Mishnah with Scripture, to which I alluded above, forms only one component in the nascent system as a whole. At hand is another, still more stunning element. The direct relationship between uttering a Torah-saying and God's revelation is made explicit in the following, which links one who utters such a saying to God:

Y. Sanhedrin 10:1:[X.E] "Given by one shepherd"—(Qoh. 12:11).
[F] Said the Holy One, blessed be He, "If you heard a teaching from an Israelite minor, and it gave pleasure to you, let it not be in your sight as if you heard it from a minor, but as if you heard it from an adult,
[G] "and let it not be as if one heard it from an adult, but as if one heard it from a sage,
[H] "and let it not be as if one heard it from a sage, but as if one heard it from a prophet,
[I] "and let it not be as if one heard it from a prophet, but as if one heard it from the shepherd,

73

[J] "and there is as a shepherd only Moses, in line with the following passage: 'Then he remembered the days of old, of Moses his servant. Where is he who brought up out of the sea the shepherds of his flock? Where is he who put in the midst of them his holy Spirit?' (Is. 63:11).

[K] "It is not as if one heard it from the shepherd but as if one heard it from the Almighty."

[L] "Given by one Shepherd"—and there is only One who is the Holy One, blessed be he, in line with that which you read in Scripture: "Hear, O Israel: the Lord our God is one Lord" (Deut. 6:4).

The status of the sage is readily inferred from this passage. He is placed on a continuum with God. The view is given below:

> Y. Sanhedrin 10:2:[IV.H] So did Ahaz say, "If there are no lambs, there will be no sheep; if there are no sheep, there will be no flock; if there is no flock, there will be no shepherd; if there is no shepherd, there will be no world; if there is no world—as it were. . . ."
>
> [I] So did Ahaz reckon, saying, "If there are no children, there will be no adults; if there are no adults, there will be no sages; if there are no sages, there will be no prophets; if there are no prophets, there will be no Holy Spirit; if there is no Holy Spirit, there will be no synagogues or schoolhouses—as it were. . . . In that case, as it were, the Holy One, blessed be He, will not let his Presence rest upon Israel."

The upshot is that the master of Torah stands and speaks for God in heaven. That is why the things he teaches—including Mishnah-traditions—enjoy the status of Torah. Accordingly, we claim too little when we associate the word Torah only with the Mishnah, or only with the Mishnah and succeeding documents. The word Torah first of all served to establish a given status. What was equivalent to the Torah became, itself, part of the Torah. Now, in the pages of the Yerushalmi, we observe yet a third step, and a most important one. The sage, the master of the Torah, now stands at the same exalted level as does the Torah itself. The nascent conceptions of Abot come to full realization in the tales we have just reviewed.

WRITTEN AND ORAL TORAH

The Mishnah is held equivalent to Scripture (Y. Hor. 3:5). But the Mishnah is not called Torah. Still, as I have pointed out, once the Mishnah entered the status of Scripture, it would take but a short step to a theory of the Mishnah as part of the revelation at Sinai —hence, oral Torah. But sages recorded in this Talmud do not appear to have taken that step.

In the Talmud at hand, we find the first glimmerings of an effort to theorize in general, not merely in detail, about how specific teachings of Mishnah relate to specific teachings of Scripture. The citing of scriptural proof-texts for Mishnaic propositions, after all, would not have caused much surprise to the framers of the Mishnah; they themselves included such passages, though not often. But what conception of the Torah underlies such initiatives, and how do Yerushalmi sages propose to explain the phenomenon of the Mishnah as a whole? The following passage gives us one statement. It refers to the assertion at M. Hag. 1:8D that the laws on cultic cleanness presented in the Mishnah rest on deep and solid foundations in the Scripture.

> Y. Hagigah 1:7:[V.A] *The laws of the Sabbath [M. 1:8B]*: R. Jonah said R. Hama bar Uqba raised the question [in reference to M. Hag. 1:8D's view that there are many verses of Scripture on cleanness], "And lo, it is written only, 'Nevertheless a spring or a cistern holding water shall be clean; but whatever touches their carcass shall be unclean' (Lev. 11:36). And from this verse you derive many laws. [So how can M. 1:8D say what it does about many verses for laws of cultic cleanness?]"
> [B] R. Zeira in the name of R. Yohanan: "If a law comes to hand and you do not know its nature, do not discard it for another one, for lo, many laws were stated to Moses at Sinai, and all of them have been embedded in the Mishnah."

The truly striking assertion appears at B. The Mishnah now is claimed to contain statements made by God to Moses. Just how these statements found their way into the Mishnah, and which passages of the Mishnah contain them, we do not know. That is hardly important, given the fundamental assertion at hand. The passage proceeds to a further, and far more consequential, proposition. It asserts that part of the Torah was written down, and part was preserved in memory and transmitted orally. In context, moreover, that distinction must encompass the Mishnah, thus explaining its origin as part of the Torah. Here is a clear and unmistakable expression of the distinction between two forms in which a single Torah was revealed and handed on at Mount Sinai, part in writing, part orally. While the passage below does not make use of the language, *Torah*-in-writing and *Torah*-by-memory, it does refer to "the written" and "the oral." I believe myself fully justified in supplying the word Torah in square brackets. The reader will note, however, that the word Torah likewise does not occur at K, L. Only when the passage reaches its climax, at M, does it break down into a number of categories—Scripture, Mishnah, Talmud, laws, lore. It there makes the additional point that *everything* comes from Moses at Sinai. So the fully articulated theory of *two Torahs* (not merely one Torah in two forms) does not reach final expression in this passage. But short of explicit allusion to *Torah*-in-writing and *Torah*-by-memory, which (so far as I am able to discern) we find mainly in the Talmud of Babylonia, the ultimate theory of Torah of formative Judaism is at hand in what follows.

Y. Hagigah 1:7:[V.D] R. Zeirah in the name of R. Eleazar: "'Were I to write for him my laws by ten thousands, they would be regarded as a strange thing' (Hos. 8:12). Now is the greater part of the Torah written down? [Surely not. The oral part is much greater.] But more abundant are the matters which are derived by exegesis from the written [Torah] than those derived by exegesis from the oral [Torah]."

[E] And is that so?

[F] But more cherished are those matters which rest upon the written [Torah] than those which rest upon the oral [Torah].

[J] R. Haggai in the name of R. Samuel bar Nahman, "Some teachings were handed on orally, and some things were handed on in writing, and we do not know which of them is the more precious. But on the basis of that which is written, 'And the Lord said to Moses, Write these words; in accordance with these words I have made a covenant with you and with Israel' (Ex. 34:27), [we conclude] that the ones which are handed on orally are the more precious."

[K] R. Yohanan and R. Yudan b. R. Simeon—One said, "If you have kept what is preserved orally and also kept what is in writing, I shall make a covenant with you, and if not, I shall not make a covenant with you."

[L] The other said, "If you have kept what is preserved orally and you have kept what is preserved in writing, you shall receive a reward, and if not, you shall not receive a reward."

[M] [With reference to Deut. 9:10: "And on them was written according to all the words which the Lord spoke with you in the mount,"] said R. Joshua b. Levi, "He could have written, 'On them,' but wrote, 'And on them.' He could have written, 'All,' but wrote, 'According to all.' He could have written, 'Words,' but wrote, 'The words.' [These then serve as three encompassing clauses, serving to include] Scripture, Mishnah, Talmud, laws, and lore. Even what an experienced student in the future is going to teach before his master already has been stated to Moses at Sinai."

[N] What is the Scriptural basis for this view?

[O] "There is no remembrance of former things, nor will there be any remembrance of later things yet to happen among those who come after" (Qoh. 1:11).

[P] If someone says, "See, this is a new thing," his fellow will answer him, saying to him, "This has been around before us for a long time."

Here we have absolutely explicit evidence that people believed part of the Torah had been preserved not in writing but orally. Linking that part to the Mishnah remains a matter of implication. But it surely comes fairly close to the surface, when we are told that the Mishnah contains Torah-traditions revealed at Sinai. From that view it requires only a small step to the allegation that the Mishnah is part of the Torah, the oral part.

At the risk of repetitiousness, let us consider yet another example in which the same notion occurs. The following passage moves from the matter of translating from the written Torah into Aramaic, so that the congregation may understand the passage, to a distinction between two *forms* of the Torah. The same discourse then goes over the ground we have just reviewed. The importance of the issue to the larger argument of this book justifies our reviewing the whole.

The first point is that when the Torah (written Scripture) is read in the synagogue, the original revelation is reenacted. God used Moses as intermediary. So the one who proclaims the Torah (in the place of God) must not be the one who then repeats Torah to the congregation (in the place of Moses). This further leads, at J, to the explicit statement that parts of the Torah were stated orally and parts in writing. Here, however, the part that is oral clearly means the Aramaic translation (Targum). In context, we need not invoke the conception of two kinds of one Torah, let alone of two Torahs constituting the one whole Torah of Moses our rabbi. That does not appear. Then, at K and following, comes the familiar discussion about two modes of one Torah. This passage then precipitates a statement of what constitutes that whole Torah, written and oral. Here, as before, "Mishnah, Talmud, and lore" join Scripture. The main point again is the assertion that whatever a sage teaches falls into the category of the Torahs of Sinai.

That point, of course, is familiar and conventional. First, what the sage says is Torah. Second, the sage cites Mishnah. Third, Mishnah is Torah.

> Y. Megillah 4:1:[II.G] R. Samuel bar R. Isaac went to a synagogue. He saw someone standing and serving as translator, leaning on a post. He said to him, "It is forbidden to you [to lean while standing]. For just as the Torah was given, originally, in fear and trembling, so we have to treat it with fear and trembling."
>
> [H] R. Haggai said R. Samuel bar R. Isaac went to a synagogue. He saw Hunah standing and serving as translator, and he had not set up anyone else in his stead [so he was both reading and translating himself]. He said to him, "It is forbidden to you, for just as it was given through an intermediary [namely, Moses] so we have to follow the custom of having an intermediary [so that the same person may not both read from the Torah and translate]."
>
> [I] R. Judah bar Pazzi went in and treated the matter as a question: "'The Lord spoke with you face to face at the mountain . . . while I stood between the Lord and you at that time, to declare to you the word of the Lord'" (Deut. 5:4–5).
>
> [J] R. Haggai said R. Samuel bar R. Isaac went into a synagogue. He saw a teacher [reading from] a translation spread out, presenting the materials from the book. He said to him, "It is forbidden to do it that way. Things which were stated orally must be presented orally. Things which were stated in writing must be presented in writing."
>
> [K] R. Haggai in the name of R. Samuel bar Nahman: "Some teachings were stated orally, and some teachings were stated in writing, and we do not know which of the two is more precious.
>
> [L] "But on the basis of that which is written, 'And the Lord said to Moses, Write these words; in accordance with these words I have made a covenant with you and with Israel' (Ex. 34:27), that is to say that the ones which are handed on orally are more precious."
>
> [M] R. Yohanan and R. Judah b. R. Simeon—one said, "[The meaning of the verse is this:] 'If you have kept what is handed on orally and if you have kept what is handed on in writing, then I shall make a covenant with you, and if not, I shall not make a covenant with you.'"
>
> [N] The other one said, "'If you have kept what is handed on orally, and if you have kept what is handed on in writing, then you will receive a reward, and if not, you will not receive a reward.'"
>
> [O] [With reference to the following verse: "And the Lord gave me the two tablets of stone written with the finger of God; and on them were all the words which the Lord had spoken with you on the mountain out of

the midst of the fire on the day of the assembly (Deut. 9:10)], said R. Joshua b. Levi, "[It is written,] 'on them,' 'and on them,' 'words,' 'the words,' 'all,' 'with all.' [These additional usages serve what purpose?]
[P] "The reference is to Scripture, Mishnah, Talmud, and lore—and even what an experienced disciple is destined to teach in the future before his master has already been stated to Moses at Sinai."
[Q] That is in line with the following verse of Scripture: "Is there a thing of which it is said, 'See, this is new'? He and his fellow will reply to him, 'It has been already in the ages before us'" (Qoh. 1:10).

Here again, the penultimate statement of the theory of the Torah of formative Judaism lies at hand. The final step is not taken here, but it is a short step indeed.

TORAH AS A WAY OF LIFE

The Talmud of the Land of Israel presents us with a succinct and exhaustive description of what the Torah-way of life demands, as opposed to the requirements of any other mode of living. What is involved, quite simply, is perpetual concentration on teachings of the Torah and their performance, to the exclusion of other thoughts and deeds. Validation of that way of life, moreover, appears in the same context. It consists in the power to perform miracles, about which, in the next section, we shall hear a good deal more. The context requires attention, as we turn to the account of how one must act to conform to the Torah's mode of living. The important passage appears at F.

Y. Taanit 3:11:[IV.B] R. Adda bar Ahvah: When he wanted it to rain, he would merely take off his sandal [as a mark of the fast, and it would rain]. If he took off both of them, the world would overflow.
[C] There was a house that was about to collapse over there, and Rab set one of his disciples in the house, until they had cleared out everything from the house. When the disciple left the house, the house collapsed.
[D] And there are those who say that it was R. Adda bar Ahvah.
[E] Sages sent and said to him, "What sort of good deeds are to your credit [that you have that much merit]?"
[F] He said to them, "In my whole life no man ever got to the synagogue in the morning before I did. I never left anybody there when I went out. I never walked four cubits without speaking words of Torah. Nor did I ever mention teachings of Torah in an inappropriate setting. I never laid out a bed and slept for a regular period of time. I never took

great strides among the associates. I never called a fellow by a nick-
name. I never rejoiced in the embarrassment of my fellow. I never
cursed my fellow when I was lying by myself in bed. I never walked
over in the marketplace to someone who owed me money.
[G] "In my entire life I never lost my temper in my household."
[H] This was meant to carry out that which is stated as follows: "I will
give heed to the way that is blameless. Oh when wilt thou come to me?
I will walk with integrity of heart within my house" (Ps. 101:2).

We should err if we construed as essentially intellectual the ideal way
of life subsumed under the word Torah. The issues are supernatural,
the outcome is salvific (as I shall argue below). Adda bar Ahvah not
only continually spoke words of Torah in appropriate places. He also
behaved in a humble, self-controlled way. Yet at the center is the notion that a person continually repeats Torah-traditions and acts in accord with them. Accordingly, study of Torah involves more than ac-
quiring information. It governs human relationships, specifically
those between master and disciple, as at Y. B.M.2:11.

But if people lived the Torah-way of life, then they had to find a
balance between the demands of the world and the requirements of
learning. They also had to know when one should set aside the processes of learning and undertake to perform what has been learned.
The following story settles the question of whether or not to set aside
Torah-learning for worldly benefit. The answer, of course, is that one
must give up gain if it would interrupt study of Torah.

> Y. Sotah 9:13:[VI.A] *And faithful men came to an end.*
> [B] Said R. Zeira, "Men faithful to the Torah."
> [C] This is in line with the following: A certain rabbi would teach Scrip-
> ture to his brother in Tyre, and when they came and called him to do
> business, he would say, "I am not going to take away from my fixed time
> to study. If the profit is going to come to me, let it come in due course
> [after my fixed time for study has ended]."

The definition of Torah as a way of life has focused our attention upon
the supernatural issue: how learning in Torah transforms the learned
man into a holy man. In the Talmud at hand, that issue comes to complete resolution. The holy man can do supernatural, that is to say,
magical, deeds. So he can save himself and others from what threat-
ens them, and, also, he can serve to save all Israel. We reach the defi-

nition, therefore, of a new category, one we have not discussed up to this point.

TORAH AS A SOURCE OF SALVATION

To define the category at hand, I point to a story that explicitly states the proposition that the Torah constitutes a source of salvation. In this story we shall see that because people observed the rules of the Torah, they expected to be saved. And if they did not observe, they accepted their punishment. So the Torah now stands for something more than revelation and a life of study, and (it goes without saying) the sage now appears as a holy, not merely a learned, man. This is because his knowledge of the Torah has transformed him. Accordingly, we deal with a category of stories and sayings about the Torah entirely different from what has gone before.

> Y. Taanit 3:8:[II.A] As to Levi ben Sisi: troops came to his town. He took a scroll of the Torah and went up to the roof and said, "Lord of the ages! If a single word of this scroll of the Torah has been nullified [in our town], let them come up against us, and if not, let them go their way."
> [B] Forthwith people went looking for the troops but did not find them [because they had gone their way].
> [C] A disciple of his did the same thing, and his hand withered, but the troops went their way.
> [D] A disciple of his disciple did the same thing. His hand did not wither, but they also did not go their way.
> [E] This illustrates the following apophthegm: You can't insult an idiot, and dead skin does not feel the scalpel.

What is interesting here is how taxa into which the word Torah previously fell have been absorbed and superseded in a new taxon. The Torah is an object: "He took a scroll. . . ." It also constitutes God's revelation to Israel: "If a single word. . . ." The outcome of the revelation is to form an ongoing way of life, embodied in the sage himself: "A disciple of his did the same thing. . . ." The sage plays an intimate part in the supernatural event: "His hand withered. . . ." Now can we categorize this story as a statement that the Torah constitutes a particular object, or a source of divine revelation, or a way of life? Yes and no. The Torah here stands not only for the things we already have catalogued. It represents one more thing which takes in all the others. Torah is a source of salvation. How so? The Torah stands for, or constitutes, the way in which the people Israel saves itself from marauders. This straightforward sense of salvation will not have surprised the author of Deuteronomy.

In the documents surveyed up to this point, we look in vain for sayings or stories that fall into such a category. True, we may take for granted that everyone always believed that, in general, Israel would be saved by obedience to the Torah. That claim would not have surprised any Israelite writers from the first prophets down through the final redactors of the Pentateuch in the time of Ezra and onward through the next seven hundred years. But, in the rabbinical corpus from the Mishnah forward, the specific and concrete assertion that by taking up the scroll of the Torah and standing on the roof of one's house, confronting God in heaven, a sage in particular could take action against the expected invasion—that kind of claim is not located, so far as I know, in any composition surveyed so far.

Still, we cannot claim that the belief that the Torah in the hands of the sage constituted a source of magical, supernatural, and hence salvific power, simply did not flourish prior, let us say, to ca. 400 C.E. We cannot show that, hence we do not know it. All we can say with assurance is that no stories containing such a viewpoint appear in any rabbinical document associated with the Mishnah. So what is critical here is not the generalized category—the genus—of conviction that the Torah serves as the source of Israel's salvation. It is the concrete assertion—the speciation of the genus—that in the hands of the sage and under conditions specified, the Torah may be utilized in pressing circumstances as Levi, his disciple, and the disciple of his disciple, used it. That is what is new.

To generalize: this stunningly new usage of Torah found in the Talmud of the Land of Israel emerges from a group of stories not readily classified in our established categories. All of these stories treat the word Torah (whether scroll, contents, or act of study) as source and guarantor of salvation. Accordingly, evoking the word Torah forms the centerpiece of a theory of Israel's history, on the one side, and an account of the teleology of the entire system, on the other. Torah indeed has ceased to constitute a specific thing or even a category or classification when stories about studying the Torah yield not a judgment as to status (i.e., praise for the learned man) but promise for supernatural blessing now and salvation in time to come.

To the rabbis the principal salvific deed was to "study Torah," by which they meant memorizing Torah-sayings by constant repetition, and, as the Talmud itself amply testifies (for some sages) profound analytic inquiry into the meaning of those sayings. The innovation now is that this act of "study of Torah" imparts supernatural power of a material character. For example, by repeating words of Torah, the sage could ward off the angel of death and accomplish other kinds of miracles as well. So Torah-formulas served as incantations. Mastery of Torah transformed the man engaged in Torah-learning into a supernatural figure, who could do things ordinary folk could not do. The category of "Torah" had already vastly expanded so that through transformation of the Torah from a concrete thing to a symbol, a Torah-scroll could be compared to a man of Torah, namely, a rabbi. Now, once the principle had been established, that salvation would come from keeping God's will in general, as Israelite holy men had insisted for so many centuries, it was a small step for rabbis to identify their particular corpus of learning, namely, the Mishnah and associated sayings, with God's will expressed in Scripture, the universally acknowledged medium of revelation.

So the single most striking phenomenon, in the Talmuds and their associated exegetical compilations, now is the vastly expanded definition of the word Torah even in its symbolized form. It was deemed appropriate to invoke that symbol for a remarkable range of purposes. But the principal instance comes first, the claim that a sage (or, disciple of a sage) himself was equivalent to a scroll of the Torah. This constituted a material comparison, not merely a symbolic metaphor:

> Y. Moed Qatan 3:7:[X.A] He who sees a disciple of a sage who has died is as if he sees a scroll of the Torah that has been burned.
> Y. Moed Qatan 3:1:[XI.I] R. Jacob bar Abayye in the name of R. Aha: "An elder who forgot his learning because of some accident which happened to him—they treat him with the sanctity owing to an ark [of the Torah]."

In the passages that follow, the notion of the sage as Torah, in the Talmud of the Land of Israel (among other rabbinic documents) stretched the bounds of the concept of Torah by showing that Scripture itself stood behind the extension and amplification of divine revelation through rational inquiry. The processes of reason, much like those undertaken in the rabbinical circles of masters and disciples, were regarded as able in themselves to generate Torah-teachings, as one thing led to another through right thinking. Whatever systematic logical analysis could derive from the Torah, that is, Scripture, was itself part of the Torah, that is, revelation. That conviction becomes explicit in the following:

> Y. Megillah 1:11:[V.L] R. Abba b. R. Pappi, R. Joshua of Sikhnin in the name of R. Levi: "Noah through reflection derived a lesson of Torah from another lesson of Torah. He said, 'It has been said to me, "And as I gave you the green plants, I give you everything" (Gen. 9:3). For what purpose has Scripture used that inclusive phrase? It serves to indicate that clean animals are for offerings.'"

Rabbis of course engaged in this sort of thinking routinely. Furthermore, they made it quite explicit that the entire corpus of rabbinical learning and tradition belonged to the category of divine revelation:

> Y. Sanhedrin 10:1:[IV.A] It is written, "Because he has despised the word of the Lord, [and has broken his commandment, that person shall be utterly cut off; his iniquity shall be upon him]" (Num. 15:31).
> [B] I know that this applies only when he despised the teaching of Torah [entirely].
> [C] How do I know that [this applies] if he denied even a single verse of Scripture, a single verse of Targum, a single argument *a fortiori*?
> [D] Scripture says, "[Because he has despised the word of the Lord,] and has broken his commandment, [that person shall be utterly cut off; his iniquity shall be upon him]" (Num. 15:31).
> [E] As to a single verse of Scripture: "[The sons of Lotan were Hori and Heman;] and Lotan's sister was Timna" (Gen. 36:22).
> [F] As to a single verse of Targum: "Laban called it Jegarsahadutha: [but Jacob called it Galeed]" (Gen. 31:47).
> [G] As to a single argument *a fortiori*: "If Cain is avenged sevenfold, [truly Lamech, seventy-sevenfold]" (Gen. 4:24).

F and G make the important and definitive point.

The notion, moreover, that the sage participated in the work of revelation, both through his memorizing of Torah-sayings and through his reasoning on them, was made explicit. The sage was holy because he knew Torah. That meant that, in his act of learning Torah, his work of memorizing and repeating sayings, and his dialectical arguments on the amplification and analysis of what he learned, the sage took over the work of Moses in receiving and interpreting the will of God. This made the sage equivalent to the prophet, indeed, superior to him. Identifying themselves with a mythic class of "scribes," sages of the Talmud stressed the superiority of their learning over the direct revelation received by prophets.

> Y. Abodah Zarah 2:7:[III.E] R. Haninah in the name of R. Idi in the name of R. Tanhum b. R. Hiyya: "More stringent are the words of the elder than the words of the prophets. For it is written, "'Do not preach"—thus they preach—"one should not preach of such things"' (Micah 2:6). And it is written, '[If a man should go about and utter wind and lies, saying,] "I will preach to you of wind and strong drink," he would be the preacher for this people!'" (Micah 2:11).
> [F] "A prophet and an elder—to what are they comparable? To a king who sent two of his senators to a certain province. Concerning one of them he wrote, 'If he does not show you my seal and signet, do not believe him.' But concerning the other one he wrote, 'Even though he does not show you my seal and signet, believe him.' So in the case of the prophet, he has had to write, 'If a prophet arises among you . . . and gives you a sign or a wonder . . .' (Deut. 13:1). But here [with regard to an elder:] '. . . according to the instructions which they give you . . .' (Deut. 17:11) [without a sign or a wonder]."

What is important here is the status imputed by the Talmud to "words of scribes," on the one side, and "the elder," on the other. Rabbis knew full well they could not provide many signs or wonders. Their principal validation lay in their role as masters of the law and clerks of the bureaucracy. So they maintained that these attainments and tasks enjoyed a status even higher than that accorded to the written Torah and the prophets. We may hardly be surprised, therefore, that sages sometimes regarded study of Torah as more important than acts of lovingkindness or other sorts of ethical actions. The master of Torah was irreplaceable.

> Y. Hagigah 1:7:[IV.A] When R. Judah would see a deceased person or a bride being praised, he would set his eyes on the disciples and say,

"Deeds come before learning. [The students should go after the crowd to praise the dead or the bride, for doing so is a religious duty.]"

[B] They voted in the upper room of the house of Aris: "Learning comes before deeds."

[C] R. Abbahu was in Caesarea. He sent R. Haninah, his son, to study Torah in Tiberias. They sent and told him, "He is doing deeds of kindness [burying the dead] there [and not studying]."

[D] He sent and wrote to him, "Is it because there are no graves in Caesarea that I sent you to Tiberias [to go around burying people]? And they have in fact taken a vote in the upper room of the house of Aris in Lud: 'Studying Torah takes precedence over deeds.'"

[E] Rabbis of Caesarea say, "That which you say applies to a case in which there is someone else who can do the deeds which are required. But if there is no one else available to do the required deeds, then doing the religious deed takes precedence over study of Torah."

[F] Once R. Hiyya, R. Yosa, R. Ammi were late in coming to see R. Eleazar. He said to them, "Where were you today?"

[G] They said to him, "We had to do a religious duty."

[H] He said to them, "And were there no others available to do it?"

[I] They said to him, "He was an alien in the country, and had no one else to bury him, [his relatives being overseas]."

The issue of the relative importance of good deeds over studying Torah was not a matter of pure theory. Concrete deeds were involved, since a disciple who went off to bury a corpse could not then spend the time reciting his sentences of the Mishnah. Only special circumstances could justify a sage's doing what less important folk could ordinarily be relied upon to carry out. It must follow that we deal not with ephemeral sayings about the relative merit of one thing over something else, but with declarations of norms. These declarations take us into the center of the Talmud's system and show us, in progression, how from the hope for salvation realized in Torah, the system moves on to the centrality of learning in Torah and the critical importance of the rabbi in the salvific process.

Y. Berakhot 2:7 [Zahavy]: When R. Simon bar Zebid died, R. Ilia came up and in regard to him expounded as follows, "Four things are essential for the world. But if they are lost they can be replaced [as we see in the following verse]. 'Surely there is a mine for silver, and a place for gold which they refine. Iron is taken out of the earth, and copper is smelted from the ore (Job 28:1–2).' If these are lost they can be replaced.

"But if a disciple of the sages dies who shall bring us his replacement? Who shall bring us his exchange? 'But where shall wisdom be found and where is the place of understanding?' (Job 28:12). 'It is hid from the eyes of all living (Job 28:21).'"

What has happened here is that the sage finds his way into the center of the Torah, so that a single symbol—the Torah—now stands for the sage and his power, as much as for the Torah and its power. In this regard the rabbinic system finds its definitive characteristic, the identification of the sage with all of its symbolic structures, the attribution to the sage of every detail of the larger system's values. Not for nothing is the result, Judaism in its formative centuries, called "rabbinic." Indeed, as the word Torah moves from scroll to symbol, it joins a much broader movement still, always toward the sage.

It had been for a long time an axiom of all forms of Judaism that, because Israel had sinned, it was punished by being given over into the hands of earthly empires; when it atoned, it was, and again would be, removed from their power. The means of atonement, reconciliation with God, were specified elsewhere as study of Torah, practice of commandments, and performance of good deeds. Why so? The answer is distinctive to the matrix of our Talmud: When Jews in general had mastered Torah, they would become sages (rabbis), just as some had already become sages —saints and holy men of a particular sort. When all Jews became sages, they would no longer lie within the power of the nations, that is, of history. Then the Messiah would come. Redemption then depended upon all Israel's accepting the yoke of the Torah. Why so? Because at that point all Israel would attain a full and complete embodiment of Torah, revelation. Thus conforming to God's will and replicating heaven on earth, Israel, as a righteous, holy community of sages, would exercise the supernatural power of Torah. They would be able as a whole to accomplish what some few saintly rabbis now could do. With access to supernatural power, redemption would naturally follow.

As I have stressed, the theory of salvation focused upon Torah addressed the circumstances of the individual as much as that of the nation. This was possible because the same factor had caused the condition of both, namely sin. Transgressing the will of God led to the fall of Israel, the destruction of the Temple. Disobedience to God's will, that is, sin, causes people to suffer and die. The angel of death has power, specifically, over those not engaged in study of Torah and performance of commandments. That view is expressed in stories indicating the belief that while a sage is repeating Torah-sayings, the angel of death cannot approach him.

> Y. Moed Qatan 3:5:[XXI.F] [Proving that while one is studying Torah, the angel of death cannot touch a person, the following is told:] A disciple of R. Hisda fell sick. He sent two disciples to him, so that they would repeat Mishnah-traditions with him. [The angel of death] turned himself before them into the figure of a snake, and they stopped repeating traditions, and [the sick man] died.
> [G] A disciple of Bar Pedaiah fell ill. He sent to him two disciples to repeat Mishnah-traditions with him. [The angel of death] turned himself before them into a kind of star, and they stopped repeating Mishnah-traditions, and he died.

Repeating Mishnah-traditions thus warded off death.

Stories were told about wonders associated with the deaths of rabbis. These validated the claim of supernatural power imputed to rabbis. A repertoire of such stories includes a list of supernatural occurrences accompanying sages' deaths, as in the following:

> Y. Abodah Zarah 3:1:[II.A] When R. Aha died, a star appeared at noon.
> [B] When R. Hanah died, the statues bowed down.
> [C] When R. Yohanan died, the icons bowed down.
> [D] They said that [this was to indicate] there were no icons like him [so beautiful as Yohanan himself].
> [E] When R. Hanina of Bet Hauran died, the Sea of Tiberias split open.
> [F] They said that [this was to commemorate the miracle that took place] when he went up to intercalate the year, and the sea split open before him.
> [G] When R. Hoshaiah died, the palm of Tiberias fell down.
> [H] When R. Isaac b. Elisheb died, seventy [infirm] thresholds of houses in Galilee were shaken down.
> [I] They said that [this was to commemorate the fact that] they [were shaky and] had depended on his merit [for the miracle that permitted them to continue to stand].

[J] When R. Samuel bar R. Isaac died, cedars of the land of Israel were uprooted.

[K] They said that [this was to take note of the fact that] he would take a branch [of a cedar] and [dance, so] praising a bride [at her wedding, and thereby giving her happiness].

[L] The rabbis would ridicule them [for lowering himself by doing so]. Said to them R. Zeira, "Leave him be. Does the old man not know what he is doing?"

[M] When he died, a flame came forth from heaven and intervened between his bier and the congregation. For three hours there were voices and thunderings in the world: "Come and see what a sprig of cedar has done for this old man!"

[N] [Further] an echo came forth and said, "Woe that Samuel b. R. R. Isaac has died, the doer of merciful deeds."

[O] When R. Yosa bar Halputa died, the gutters ran with blood in Laodicea.

[P] They said [that the reason was] that he had given his life for the rite of circumcision.

[Q] When R. Abbahu died, the pillars of Caesarea wept.

[R] The [gentiles] said [that the reason was] that [the pillars] were celebrating. The Israelites said to them, "And do those who are distant [such as yourselves] know why those who are near [we ourselves] are raising a cry?"

Y. Abodah Zarah 3:1:[II.BB] One of the members of the patriarchate died, and the [burial] cave folded over [and received the bier], so endangering the lives [of those who had come to bury him]. R. Yosé went up and took leave [of the deceased], saying "Happy is a man who has left this world in peace."

[CC] When R. Yosé died, the castle of Tiberias collapsed, and members of the patriarchate were rejoicing. R. Zeira said to them, "There is no similarity [between this case and the miracle described at BB]. The peoples' lives were endangered, here no one's life was endangered. In that case, no pagan worship was removed, while here, an idol was uprooted [so, consequently, the event described in BB was not a miracle, while the event described here was a miracle and a sign of divine favor]."

What is important in the foregoing is the linkage between the holy deeds of the sage and the miracles performed at their demise. The sages' merit, attained through study of Torah or through acts of saintliness and humility (despite mastery of Torah), was demonstrated for all to see. So the sage was not merely a master of Torah. But his mastery of Torah laid the foundations for all the other things he was.

Thus far we have seen that the Talmud maintains that through his mastery of the Torah the sage exercised magical-supernatural powers whereby to reward his friends and punish his enemies. We have now to show that the supernatural status accorded to the person of the sage endowed his deeds with normative, therefore revelatory, power. What the sage did had the status of Torah-law. The sage therefore was the model of the fulfilled law, the human embodiment of the Torah. That mundane view has to be joined to the otherworldly notion of the sage as a holy man. For what made the sage distinctive was his combination of this-worldly authority and power and otherworldly influence. The clerk in the court and the holy man on the rooftop in the Talmud's view were one and the same: Torah incarnate. Given the fundamental point of insistence of the Talmud, that the salvation of Israel will derive from keeping the Torah, the Talmud had no choice but to preserve the tight union between salvation and law, the magical power of the sage and his lawgiving authority. We turn now to spell out this definitive trait of the system as a whole, as exemplified in the Yerushalmi. To state matters simply: If the sage exercised supernatural power as a kind of living Torah, his very deeds, as much as his word, served to reveal Torah-law.

The capacity of the sage himself to participate in the process of Torah-revelation is illustrated in two types of materials. First of all, tales told about rabbis' behavior on specific occasions immediately are translated into rules for the entire community to keep. Accordingly, he was a source not merely of good example but of prescriptive law, law of the status of the Torah's rules:

> Y. Abodah Zarah 5:4:[III.X] R. Aha went to Emmaus, and he ate dumpling [prepared by Samaritans].
> [Y] R. Jeremiah ate leavened bread prepared by them.
> [Z] R. Hezekiah ate their locusts prepared by them.
> [AA] R. Abbahu prohibited Israelite use of wine prepared by them.

These reports—and the Talmud presents hundreds of them—of rabbis' actions enjoyed the same authority, as abstract statements of the law on eating Samaritans' cooking, as did citations of traditions in the names of great authorities of old or of the day. A person's conduct served as a norm, if the person was a sage of sufficient standing. It would then come to restatement as an abstract law.

Far more common in the Talmud are instances in which the deed of a rabbi is adduced as an authoritative precedent for the law under discussion. It was everywhere taken for granted that what a rabbi did, he did because of his mastery of the law. Even though a formulation of the law was not in hand, a tale about a rabbi's actual behavior constituted adequate guidance for formulating the law itself. So from the practice of an authority, a law might be framed quite independently of the person of the sage. The sage then functioned as a lawgiver, like Moses. Among many instances of that mode of generating law are the following:

> Y. Abodah Zarah 3:11:[II.A] Gamaliel Zuga was walking along, leaning on the shoulder of R. Simeon b. Laqish. They came across an image. [B] He said to him, "What is the law as to passing before it?" [C] He said to him, "Pass before it, but close [your] eyes." [D] R. Isaac was walking along, leaning on the shoulder of R. Yohanan. They came across an idol before the council building. [E] He said to him, "What is the law as to passing before it?" [F] He said to him, "Pass before it, but close [your] eyes." [G] R. Jacob bar Idi was walking along, leaning upon R. Joshua b. Levi. They came across a procession in which an idol was carried. He said to him, "Nahum, the most holy man, passed before this idol, and will you not pass by it? Pass before it but close your eyes."
>
> Y. Abodah Zarah 2:2:[III.FF] R. Aha had chills and fever. [They brought him] a medicinal drink prepared from the phallus of Dionysian revelers [thus Jastrow, *Dictionary*, I 400 B]. But he would not drink it. They brought it to R. Jonah, and he did drink it. Said R. Mana, "Now if R. Jonah, the patriarch, had known what it was, he would never have drunk it."
> [GG] Said R. Huna, "That is to say, 'They do not accept healing from something that derives from an act of fornication.'"

What is striking is GG, the restatement of the story as a law. The example of a rabbi showed how one should live a truly holy life. The requirements went far beyond the measure of the law, extending to refraining from deeds of a most commonplace sort. The example of rabbinical virtue, moreover, was adduced explicitly to account for his supernatural or magical power. There was no doubt in people's minds, therefore, that rabbis could do the amazing things people said they did because they embodied the Torah and exercised its supernatural or magical power.

The correlation between learning and teaching, on the one side, and supernatural power or recognition, on the other, is not our invention. It is made explicit in the following:

> Y. Ketubot 12:3:[VII.A] R. Yosa fasted eighty fasts in order to see R. Hiyya the Elder [in a dream]. He finally saw him, and his hands trembled and his eyes grew dim.
> [B] Now if you say that R. Yosa was an unimportant man, [and so was unworthy of such a vision, that is not the case]. For a weaver came before R. Yohanan. He said to him, "I saw in my dream that the heaven fell, and one of your disciples was holding it up."
> [C] He said to him, "Will you know him [when you see him]?"
> [D] He said to him, "When I see him, I shall know him." Then all of his disciples passed before him, and he recognized R. Yosa.
> [E] R. Simeon b. Laqish fasted three hundred fasts in order to have a vision of R. Hiyya the Elder, but he did not see him.
> [F] Finally he began to be distressed about the matter. He said, "Did he labor in learning of Torah more than I?"
> [G] They said to him, "He brought Torah to the people of Israel to a greater extent than you have, and not only so, but he even went into exile [to teach on a wider front]."
> [H] He said to them, "And did I not go into exile too?"
> [I] They said to him, "You went into exile only to learn, but he went into exile to teach others."

This story shows that the storyteller took for granted the correlation between mastery of Torah-sayings and supernatural power—in this case, visions of the deceased. That is why Simeon b. Laqish complained, E–F, that he had learned as much Torah as the other, and so should likewise be able to conjure the dead. The greater supernatural power of the other then was explained in terms of the latter's superior service to the Torah. The upshot is that the sage was made a magician by Torah-learning and could save Israel through Torah, source of the most powerful magic of all.

The clearest picture of the theory of salvation through Torah, in the Talmud of the Land of Israel, is to be found in the sages' reading of Scripture. Specifically, the world view retrojected by them upon the heroes of ancient Israel most clearly reveals the sages' view of the Torah as a source of salvation. The Talmud's framers took for granted that the world they knew in the fourth century had flourished a thousand and more years earlier. The values they embodied and the supernatural powers they fantasized for themselves predictably were projected backward onto biblical figures. Biblical and talmudic authorities lived on a single plane of being, in a single age of shared discourse; the Mishnah and associated documents amply restated propositions held for all time and proved in Scripture too.

What is important is the theory of salvation given its clearest statement by the anachronistic reading of Scripture characteristic of talmudic sages. Especially striking in the utilization of the Torah in the rabbinical doctrine of salvation is the blurring of boundaries between the nation and the individual. Formerly, individuals required one kind of salvation from one set of problems, the nation a different kind of salvation from another. Now the Torah, as source of salvation, was made to serve both sets of needs. Let me explain. Suffering afflicted both individual and nation. Catastrophe in the form of a historical, onetime event, such as the destruction of the Temple, was juxtaposed with personal suffering and death. Accordingly, while the troubles the nation and its people must be saved from were many, the mode of salvation would be one and the same. The consequence for the theory of salvation was this. The Torah might protect a person from suffering or death, and the Torah might also (in due course) save Israel from its subjugation to the nations of the world. So for both the Jewish individual and Israelite society, Torah would save Israel *from* sin and suffering, *for* a life of Torah in heaven as much as on earth. How so? Since heaven was conceived in the model of earth, so that the analysis of traditions on earth corresponded to the discovery of the principles of creation (as made explicit in Genesis Rabbah, below), the full realization of the teachings of Torah on earth, in the life of Israel, would transform Israel into a replica of heaven on earth.

We deal, therefore, with a doctrine of salvation in which the operative symbol, namely, Torah, and the determinative deed, namely, Torah-learning, defined not only how to attain salvation but also the very nature of that salvation. The system thus was whole and coherent. Entering it at any point, we find ourselves at once within the structure as a whole. We enter a great, well-ordered hall, the inside of a world fully visible all at once, a kind of Globe Theater of Torah and of Israel. It is important, then, to recognize, as we do, that the profound issues confronting Israelite existence, national and personal alike, here and now, were framed in terms of Torah and resolved through the medium of Torah. Stated simply: salvation would come from Torah, and Torah defined the nature of salvation.

What was the rabbis' view of salvation? Seeing Scripture in their own image, they took the position that the Torah of old, its supernatural power and salvific promise, in their own day continued to endure among themselves. In consequence, the promise of salvation contained in every line of Scripture was to be kept in each deed of learning and obedience to the Torah effected under their auspices. So in their eyes they carried forward, in their own persons, the promise of salvation for Israel contained within the written Torah of old.

In locating sages in the written Torah, therefore, the Talmud's sages implicitly stated their view of themselves as the continuation of the sanctified way of life. It followed that the pattern and promise of salvation contained in the Torah inhered in their own lives. That is the meaning of the explicit reading of the present into the past, the implicit arrogation of the hope of the past to the salvific heroes of the present: themselves.

To state matters simply, if David, King of Israel, was like a rabbi today, then a rabbi today represents the son of David who was to come as King of Israel. It is not surprising, therefore, that among the many biblical heroes whom the talmudic rabbis treated as sages, principal and foremost was David himself, now made into a messianic rabbi or a rabbinical Messiah. He was the sage of the Torah, the avatar and model for the sages of their own time. That view was made explicit. If a rabbi was jealous to have his traditions cited in his own name, it was because that was David's view as well. In more general terms, both David and Moses are represented as students of Torah, just like the disciples and sages of the current time.

> Y. Sheqalim 2:4:[V.O] David himself prayed for mercy for himself, as it is said, "Let me dwell in thy tent for ever! Oh to be safe under the shelter of thy wings, *selah*" (Ps. 61:4).
> [P] And did it enter David's mind that he would live for ever?
> [Q] But this is what David said before the Holy One, blessed be he, "Lord of the world, may I have the merit that my words will be stated in synagogues and schoolhouses."

[R] Simeon b. Nazira in the name of R. Isaac said, "Every disciple in whose name people cite a teaching of law in this world—his lips murmur with him in the grave, as it is said, 'Your kisses are like the best wine that goes down smoothly, gliding over lips of those that sleep' (Song. 7:9).

[S] "Just as in the case of a mass of grapes, once a person puts his finger in it, forthwith even his lips begin to smack, so the lips of the righteous, when someone cites a teaching of law in their names—their lips murmur with them in the grave."

Y. Berakhot 1:1 (Zahavy) [XII.O] "I will awaken the dawn" (Ps. 57:8)—I will awaken the dawn; the dawn will not awaken me.

[P] David's [evil] impulse tried to seduce him [to sin]. And it would say to him, "David. It is the custom of kings that they sleep until the third hour [of the day]. And you say, At midnight I rise." And [David] used to say [in reply], "[I rise early] because of thy righteous ordinances (Ps. 119:62)."

[Q] And what would David do? R. Phineas in the name of R. Eleazar b. R. Menahem [said], "[He used to take a harp and lyre and set them at his bedside. And he would rise at midnight and play them so that the associates of Torah should hear. And what would the associates of Torah say? 'If David involves himself with Torah, how much more so should we.' We find that all of Israel was involved in Torah [study] on account of David."

Y. Horayot 3:5:[I.E] R. Yohanan, "All these forty days that Moses served on the mountain, he studied the Torah but forgot it. In the end it was given to him as a gift. All this why? So as to bring the stupid students back to their studies [when they become discouraged]."

This long extract shows us how the Talmud's authorities readily saw their own concerns in biblical statements attributed to David. As above, at Y. San. 2:5.IV, "water" meant "a teaching of Torah." "Three mighty men" were of course judges. At issue was whether or not the decision was to be stated in David's own name—and so removed from the authoritative consensus of sages. David exhibits precisely those concerns for the preservation of his views in his name that, in earlier sections, we saw attributed to rabbis. All of this, as we have noted, fully reveals the rabbis' deeper convictions when we remember that David *the rabbi* also was in everyone's mind David *the Messiah*. The upshot of these stories is that the sage does not merely set a good example, nor does he exercise merely a useful social role through teaching and exemplifying the Torah. The sage turns out to constitute a liminal figure standing between heaven and earth. When the Messiah comes, he too will be a sage. So the sage here and now is like the Messiah who is to come. The sage here and now embodies the Torah.

At this point the reader will have observed a striking shift in discourse. We began by talking about the Torah as a source of salvation. But we end by speaking about the sage as Torah incarnate. The simple fact, therefore, is that when we reach the Talmud of the Land of Israel (and documents of its circle and viewpoints), we cannot speak about the Torah by itself, but only about Torah as abstract symbol, the instrument and effect of the myth of the sage. That is to say, the word Torah stands for a symbolic abstraction integral to the larger myth of the sage as Torah incarnate: "in our likeness." The myth of the Torah (the two Torahs making up the one whole Torah of Moses our rabbi) stands subordinate to a more encompassing myth, of which it forms an important component. True, our survey of Abot turned up no explicit statement of that position. But, as we shall now observe, after studying Abot we cannot be surprised by the present conclusion.

THE TALMUDIC THEORY
OF THE TORAH

The key to the Talmud's theory of the Torah lies in its conception of the sage, to which that theory is subordinate. Once the sage reaches his full apotheosis as Torah incarnate, then, but only then, the Torah becomes (also) a source of salvation in the present concrete formulation of the matter. That is why we traced the doctrine of the Torah in the salvific process by elaborate citation of stories about sages, living Torahs, exercising the supernatural power of the Torah, and serving, like the Torah itself, to reveal God's will. Since the sage embodied the Torah and gave the Torah, the Torah naturally came to stand for the principal source of Israel's salvation, not merely a scroll, on the one side, or a source of revelation, on the other.

The history of the symbolization of the Torah proceeds from its removal from the framework of material objects, even from the limitations of its own contents, to its transformation into something quite different and abstract, quite distinct from the document and its teachings. The Torah stands for this something more, specifically, when it comes to be identified with a living person, the sage, and endowed with those particular traits that the sage claimed for himself. While we cannot say that the process of symbolization leading to the pure abstraction at hand moved in easy stages, we may still point to the stations that had to be passed in sequence. The word Torah reached the apologists for the Mishnah in its long-established meanings: Torah-scroll, contents of the Torah-scroll. But even in the Mishnah itself, these meanings provoked a secondary development, status of Torah as distinct from other (lower) status, hence, Torah-teaching in contradistinction to scribal-teaching. With that small and simple step, the Torah ceased to denote only a concrete and material thing—a scroll and its contents. It now connoted an abstract matter of status. And once made abstract, the symbol entered a secondary history beyond all limits imposed by the concrete object, including its specific teachings, the Torah-scroll.

I believe that Abot stands at the beginning of this process. In the history of the word Torah as abstract symbol, a metaphor serving to sort out one abstract status from another regained concrete and material reality of a new order entirely. For the message of Abot, as we saw, was that the Torah served the sage. How so? The Torah indicated who was a sage and who was not. Accordingly, the apology of Abot for the Mishnah was that the Mishnah contained things sages had said. What sages said formed a chain of tradition extending back to Sinai. Hence it was equivalent to the Torah. The upshot is that words of sages enjoyed the status of the Torah. The small step beyond, I think, was to claim that what sages said was Torah, *as much as what Scripture said was Torah.* And, a further small step (and the steps need not have been taken separately or in the order here suggested) moved matters to the position that there were two forms in which the Torah reached Israel: one [Torah] in writing, the other [Torah] handed on orally, that is, in memory. The final step, fully revealed in the Talmud at hand, brought the conception of Torah to its logical conclusion: what the sage said was in the status of the Torah, was Torah, because the sage was Torah incarnate. So the abstract symbol now became concrete and material once more. We recognize the many, diverse ways in which the Talmud stated that conviction.

Every passage in which knowledge of the Torah yields power over this world and the next, capacity to coerce to the sage's will the natural and supernatural worlds alike, rests upon the same viewpoint.

The Talmud's theory of the Torah carries us through several stages in the processes of the symbolization of the word Torah. First transformed from something material and concrete into something abstract and beyond all metaphor, the word Torah finally emerged once more in a concrete aspect, now as the encompassing and universal mode of stating the whole doctrine, all at once, of Judaism in its formative age.

5

The Compilations
of Scriptural Exegesis

THE FIRST SEQUENCE:
EXEGESIS OF THE PENTATEUCH,
VERSE BY VERSE, IN THE NAME OF
MISHNAH-AUTHORITIES (TANNAIM):
MEKHILTA, SIFRA, SIFRE NUMBERS,
AND SIFRE DEUTERONOMY

The compilations of exegesis of scriptural verses, known as mid-rashim, are constructed of units of discourse taxonomically parallel to the compilations of exegesis of Mishnah-units. These compilations fall into three groups. First come those, dealing solely with the Penta-teuch, which consist of verse-by-verse, sometimes phrase-by-phrase, exposition and amplification of Scripture's meaning. These I call the first sequence, solely for purposes of classification. We have no basis for determining the time at which the several documents reached closure. Second come collections of exegesis, also dealing only with pentateuchal books, in which verse-by-verse reading of passages is in-terspersed with units of discourse of a more discursive character. In these units, a specific topic or theme is investigated through citation of verses from various biblical books. These collections, here called the second sequence, expound Genesis and Leviticus. The third and last sequence comprises compilations of exegesis predominantly of a discursive, hence more theological or philosophical, order. In this last set of collections, thematic discourse overspreads the whole, so that explanation of individual verses, phrases, or words is subordinated to the exposition of a basic theme.

In treating the uses of the word Torah in these diverse kinds of composition, I mean only to advance the required survey. I make no claim that these compositions differ in fundamental viewpoint from the other writings of the rabbinic canon framed around the Mishnah, or that they derive from a different institutional or social setting. While both of those possibilities may in time demand exploration, for the modest purpose at hand they need only be recorded.

For the first group we have the advantage of complete concordances, while for the second and third, I have had to rely upon the expedient of turning pages and recording occurrences. Such an on-site inspection, by definition, is less reliable than resort to a complete concordance; so, when concordances become available, the survey of the second and third groups will have to be redone. I am inclined to doubt, however, that fundamental revision will be needed.

THE TORAH AS A PARTICULAR THING

1. *Mekhilta*. Mekhilta's references pertain to specific chapters and verses of Exodus. "A scroll of Torah," meaning a particular thing, occurs at Mekh. to Ex. 17:14; 18:25. When we find, "the Torah is fine" (Mekh. to Ex. 19:18), the reference is to the physical condition or aspect of the Torah as an object. "Reading in the Torah" (Mekh. to Ex. 13:9) is to read in the scroll of Torah in particular.

2. *Sifra*. The Torah-scroll's presence distinguishes Israelites from idolaters (Behuqotai 8:10).

3. *Sifre Numbers*. "This Torah-scroll" (Sifre Num. 141) refers not to the object, but to the teachings.

4. *Sifre Deuteronomy*. The Samaritan scribes made a counterfeit Torah (Sifre Deut. 56), meaning that they wrote in the scroll something that does not belong or omitted something that does. A governor burned the Torah (Sifre Deut. 307), meaning a scroll. When Moses gave the Torah, it did not lack a single letter (Sifre Deut. 357). Moses wrote the entire Torah (Sifre Deut. 1). He did not change it (Sifre Deut. 20).

THE TORAH AS REVELATION

1. *Mekhilta*. A phrase like "The Torah has said," or "has taught," uses the word Torah to refer to a corpus of revelation. Whenever we find this phrase or its equivalents, the cited Torah-text is always a verse of Scripture, explicitly cited or not. We do not find the equivalent of what we saw in the Yerushalmi, that is, use of the word Torah applied to a Targum or Mishnah passage. The meaning of revelation is

imputed to the word at Mekh. to Ex. 12:2; 13:9, 13, 17; 19:8; 20:3; 21:1, 6, 11, 17, 19, 26; 22:6, 12, 22; 23:2, 7, 11, 19. "Words of Torah" as revealed doctrine occurs at Mekh. to Ex. 15:22, 25, 26 (all in the sense of revelation); 20:12 ("words of Torah" are expounded); 22:3. "Israel will be strengthened by words of Torah, which will be given through Moses' hands" (Mekh. to Ex. 17:11) seems to me to refer to Torah as revelation. "Words of Torah" at Mekh. to Ex. 13:1; 20:12 means Torah teachings and how they are interpreted. "Torah is light," Mekh. to Ex. 13:18, surely uses the word to mean divine revelation. Right action taught by the Torah appears at Mekh. to Ex. 12:11; 13:22; 21:19. "The Torah will be forgotten" refers to the contents of revelation, Mekh. to Ex. 12:26. "Torah" as the source of various doctrines ("From the Torah") serves at Mekh. to Ex. 15:1. "The Torah is called . . ." refers not to the scroll but the revelation, so Mekh. to Ex. 15:16, 17. When we find a reference to carrying out "the whole Torah" (Mekh. to Ex. 15:26; 16:4) the meaning is the entirety of revealed law. "Why were the Ten Commandments not stated at the start of the Torah" (Mekh. to Ex. 20:2) treats "Torah" as the compilation of various passages of revelation.

When, finally, we find reference to what is "in the Torah," the meaning is "in the contents of revelation." So Mekh. to Ex. 12:1, 5, 6; 13:9; 15:9–10, 22; 17:9; 18:1; 19:10, 11; 21:15, 16, 17, 19, 25; 22:18. Along these same lines, "all the relevant rules or statements that are in the Torah" and parallel usages refer to Torah as a corpus of revealed truth, at Mekh. to Ex. 12:1, 21, 22, 49; 15:1; 20:1, 2, 22; 21:1, 18, 20; 22:5, 10, 24; 23:19. When we hear about "a fence for the Torah" the context always dictates the simple meaning "for the observance of rules in the Torah" as at Mekh. to Ex. 12:8. When Ex. 18:20 refers to *torot*, Mekh. interprets by using the word "instructions" or "decisions."

The phrase "commandments which are in the Torah" speaks of Torah as revelation, as source of right law and doctrine—again invariably with regard to Scripture, as at Mekh. to Ex. 12:49.

"Torah" is compared to "the Land of Israel" and "the world to come" at Mekh. to Ex. 20:20. "Torah of the Lord" is parallel to the covenant, Mekh. to Ex. 13:17, and both instances seem to use the word to mean revelation.

"Torah" as revelation ("Torah was given . . .") occurs explicitly at Mekh. to Ex. 13:17, 18; 16:1, 4; 18:1, 8; 19:2, 4, 10, 11, 17; 20:15, 20, 21; 21:14; 22:19; 23:19. Israel's "accepting" the Torah when it was "given" occurs at Mekh. to Ex. 15:8, 13; 20:2, 15. "Proclaim this Torah" (Mekh. to Ex. 23:14) means "declare revelation." "The noise or sound of Torah at Sinai" (Mekh. to Ex. 18:25) refers to the revelation of the Torah.

2. *Sifra.* Torah as a revelation and source of divinely revealed truth occurs in such familiar usages as "the Torah has said" or "it is stated in the Torah," as in the following passages: Nedabah II:4; Saw V:1; Qedoshim 1:10; III:9; X:1; 9:6; Behar 9:3; Qedoshim 10:6. "Words of the Torah" means revealed rules at Shemini 7:12; "stated in the Torah" occurs at Nedabah 2:1, 4; 10:7; X:6; 12:2; Hobah 3:6; IV:7, 8; VII:2; Saw 4:6; Mesora 5:9; Ahare 13:10; Qedoshim I:10; 9:11, 13; 11:10, 24; Emor III:12; Behuqota II:1; Nedabah I:6; Ahare 5:8; Qedoshim 9:7, 11, 12, 14; 10:1, 3. "Torah" applies or decrees a rule at Mesora I:4, V:12, 5:12; Ahare 11:2; Behar 9:3.

"The principles of the Torah"—the main points of revelation—occur at Qedoshim I:1. So too, "the great principle in the Torah" is at Qedoshim 4:12.

The Torah was "given" or revealed, so Behuqotai 8:12. It was rejected by the nations, so Behuqotai 2:5; 3:6; Ahare 13:14. The "Torah of Moses, your servant" refers to revelation, at Ahare II:4; 2:9; IV:6.

3. *Sifre Numbers.* Once again we categorize as meaning revelation the usage of the word Torah to mean a source of right doctrine. When David, King of Israel, sought "Torah" (Sifre Num. 119), it was knowledge of God's will—something to be learned and obeyed. Other instances in which "Torah" gives right information are as follows: Sifre Num. 134, 152, 154; "the Torah has stated" is at Sifre Num. 3, 23, 35, 107, 112, 115, 142, 153, 156, 160. "In all of the Torah we find (or: do not find) a given fact"—so Sifre Num. 1, 2, 107, 108, 111, 118. Further references to "in the Torah" (always to specific verses of Scripture) appear at Sifre Num. 1, 2, 8, 10, 11, 14, 15, 32, 40, 58, 64, 73, 78, 93, 107, 111, 112, 123, 134, 141, 142, 143, 153. Allusions to "which is/are in the Torah" are found at Sifre Num. 1, 2, 8, 14, 15, 16, 23, 24, 31, 58, 71, 73, 76, 107, 108, 109, 110, 112, 113, 115, 123, 132, 142, 143, 153. An expert "in the innermost chambers of the Torah" knows how to interpret revelation (Sifre Num. 116). Moses stated "the entire Torah" at the dictation of the Holy One (Sifre Num. 112). "When the Torah goes forth from his mouth . . ." (Sifre Num. 119) refers to revealed truth.

4. *Sifre Deuteronomy.* "The Torah was created for the glory of Is-

rael" (Sifre Deut. 47). When we see the word Torah in context referring to a source of authoritative truth, we interpret the usage to mean revelation—hence the contents of the Torah-scroll. The Torah "says," "speaks," "teaches," "selects certain words," and the like, at Sifre Deut. 43, 51, 71, 106, 181, 220, 269, 295; 16, 34, 35, 42, 54, 122, 145; 115, 126, 142, 222, 225, 270. "Words of Torah," meaning teachings of Scripture, occurs at the following: Sifre Deut. 41, 45, 46, 48, 87, 306. "That which is written in the Torah" and parallels appear at Sifre Deut. 113, 148, 155, 175, 178, 201, 241, 269, 273, 288, 293, 323, 336, 347; "which is in the Torah," Sifre Deut. 12, 27, 44, 80, 190, 228, 243, 295, 308.

"Some say that the Torah does not derive from Heaven," Sifre Deut. 102. But God gave Torah to Israel through Moses, so Sifre Deut. 305; from Heaven, Sifre Deut. 306, 311, 314, 343, 345; in four languages, Sifre Deut. 343. The giving of the Torah, that is, revelation, is referred to at Sifre Deut. 76, 343.

The essence of the Torah is in the laws, Sifre Deut. 317. But other doctrines are derived "from the Torah," meaning from Scripture, Sifre Deut. 43, 47, 156, 237.

Torah falls into the same classification as the Land of Israel and the world to come, at Sifre Deut. 32. Torah was created before anything else, so Sifre Deut. 37. These assertions seem out of phase here.

TORAH AS A PARTICULAR ACT.
AS GENERIC

1. *Mekhilta.* "Torah" requires a blessing, hence the meaning can only be "the study of Torah," so Mekh. to Ex. 13:1. "Those who study Torah," meaning sages, is found at Mekh. to Ex. 18:12. "The father teaches the son Torah," so Mekh. to Ex. 20:12. Further references to the act of Torah-study or Torah-teaching are as follows: Mekh. to Ex. 15:27 ("occupied with words of Torah"); Ex. 18:22; 19:5; 22:3. "The Torah of the Lord" is to be studied, Mekh. to Ex. 13:9. People who have abandoned "works of Torah" for three days have neglected the act of Torah-study for that period (Mekh. to Ex. 15:22; 17:1, 8). Neglect of "the Torah" meaning Torah-study also is at Mekh. to Ex. 13:17; 16:33; 18:25. Explicit reference to Torah-study (*Talmud-Torah*) further occurs at Mekh. to Ex. 13:9, 13; 14:13; 18:20; 18:25; 19:1.

Reading "in the Torah" means study of Scripture in particular, at Mekh. to Ex. 20:6.

The generic sense of *torah* as a governing rule appears only once, at Mekh. to Ex. 15:1.

2. *Sifra.* We find studying or teaching Torah at Emor I:6; engaging or occupied in [study of] Torah, at Shemini 29; laboring in Torah, at Behuqotai I:1, 2.

"Torah" in the sense of the rule governing a given category occurs at Shemini 12:5; Saw 18:3, 9; Negaim 16:12; Mesora I:1; 5:16; Saw 2:1, 2; IV:1; V:1.

3. *Sifre Numbers.* "Torah" refers to the act of study or teaching, at Sifre Num. 78, 115, 119. "Torah" gave knowledge to sages, so Sifre Num. 134. "Those who learn [or study] the Torah" appears at Sifre Num. 42. Enjoying God's favor in Torah-study (Sifre Num. 41) means that one masters traditions with ease. One who loves "the Torah" (Sifre Num. 42, 78) presumably enjoys learning Torah-traditions.

4. *Sifre Deuteronomy.* Torah is something learned or taught, particularly by the father, at Sifre Deut. 14, 32, 34, 41 (not to be done in order to become rich), 42, 46, 48 (as equivalent to performing a religious duty), 62, 79, 80, 305, 306, 321, 352, 357. Torah may not only be learned, but also forgotten, so Sifre Deut. 48, 160, 306. The process is through the give-and-take of argument (Sifre Deut. 321). "Words of Torah" to be learned and taught form the center of discourse at Sifre Deut. 48. One must not leave off learning words of Torah, Sifre Deut. 174. In matters of learning words of Torah all are equal (Sifre Deut. 48, 161). One learns by close attention (Sifre Deut. 335). "Study of Torah" further occurs at Sifre Deut. 44 (comparing study to other religious duties), 106, 336. The tribe of Issachar is distinguished by its knowledge of the Torah (Sifre Deut. 54).

"The rule governing . . ." is the generic sense at Sifre Deut. 43.

TORAH AS INDICATOR OF STATUS

1. *Mekhilta.* The distinction between a rule derived from a statement in the (written) Torah and one based on the authority of others (e.g., scribes) occurs at Mekh. to Ex. 13:13. "Sons of Torah" appear as analogous to sages at Mekh. to Ex. 18:12.

2. *Sifra.* The distinction between teachings of Torah and teachings of scribes plays a role at Behar 4:5; Shemini VII:12; 8:5; Zab. 4:6 and Emor X:10, 11.

3. *Sifre Numbers*. There are three crowns: those of the king, the priest, and the Torah (Sifre Num. 119). By analogy to "king" and "priest," "Torah" must signify a matter of status. "Sitting in the Sanhedrin and teaching words of Torah" (Sifre Num. 78, 80) seems to me to connote people in the status of authoritative judges.

A rule "based on the authority of the Torah" is distinguished from one based on some other authority, at Sifre Num. 8, 73, 116, 150.

4. *Sifre Deuteronomy*. There are heroes of the Torah (Sifre Deut. 321, 347). "Words of Torah" are conventionally balanced against "words of scribes," at Sifre Deut. 115, 154. But "words of Torah" are set against "words of prophets" (Sifre Deut. 218), in which instance Torah refers only to the Pentateuch.

Some rules derive from the Torah, others do not (Sifre Deut. 103, 104, 156, a religious duty deriving from the Torah).

WRITTEN AND ORAL TORAH

1. *Mekhilta*. This distinction does not appear. Mekhilta makes no unambiguous reference to the myth of the two Torahs of Sinai.

2. *Sifra*. The use of the plural, *Torot*, refers to two Torahs, one in writing, the other oral, so Behuqotai 8:12. But Israel was given not two, but *many* Torahs (*Torot*), so Aqiba at the same passage.

3. *Sifre Numbers*. No passage alludes to the myth of the two Torahs.

4. *Sifre Deuteronomy*. Sifre Deut. 351 states that two Torahs were given to Israel: one in writing, one transmitted through memorization. This reference is quite unambiguous.

TORAH AS A WAY OF LIFE

1. *Mekhilta*. When "Torah" is treated as equivalent to "covenant," as at Mekh. to Ex. 12:6, I think the meaning encompasses the whole way of life, rather than solely "study of Torah" or revelation in general. "Israel cannot survive without Torah," Mekh. to Ex. 17:8, uses the word in the broadest possible sense. Likewise, "bringing someone to the Torah" means to convert him to the way of life of the Torah, not merely to inform, but to change, the person, as at Mekh. to Ex. 18:1, 8. I see the same meaning in the phrase "to give one's life for the Torah" at Mekh. to Ex. 15:1. The conviction that "Torah" is the source of Israel's merit seems to me to utilize the word in a sense

broader than Israel's act of study of divine revelation, as at Mekh. to Ex. 15:2, 13: Israel builds the sanctuary because of the merit gained through "Torah." This phrase refers to the Torah as revelation, the act of study, and the entire way of life. I find a similar sense in Torah as booty at Mekh. to Ex. 20:15. Torah as a source of merit appears at Mekh. to Ex. 14:28–29. "Giving one's life for the Torah" (Mekh. to Ex. 15:1) encompasses this broader sense as well: doctrine and action alike.

It does not seem farfetched to discern in the claim that Israel cannot survive without Torah an adumbration of the conviction that Torah is a source of salvation. So too, when Israel gains merit "through Torah," the meaning may transcend the narrow limit of gaining reward for studying revelation. Yet the rich and full expression of the salvific power of the Torah, such as we find in the Yerushalmi's pertinent statements, does not seem to me to be present in the Mekhilta.

2. *Sifra.* A gentile who "does [carries out] the Torah" surely conforms to the holy way of life (Ahare 13:13), so too Qedoshim 8:3; 10:6, 7; Behuqotai 2:4. This is explicit at Qedoshim 10:6–7, which equates "carrying out the Torah" with doing the will of one's Father in heaven. Those who "deny the Torah" reject revelation and the whole holy way, so Ahare 13:14; Behuqotai 2:5; 3:6. "Bringing sinners back to the Torah" restores their life-pattern to what it should be (Shemini 38; Ahare 8:10).

3. *Sifre Numbers.* When, at Sifre Num. 111, "the covenant" is identified with "Torah," "Torah" stands for the entire way of life, not merely facts or authoritative rules. "Torah" brings a person eternal life, so Sifre Num. 119. When Sifre Num. 41 refers to "the light of the Torah" the meaning is surely figurative and encompassing. "All the words of this Torah" (Sifre Num. 161) are to be kept, observed, or carried out—hence shaping a way of life. "Paying no attention to the teachings of the Torah in one's lifetime" (Sifre Num. 112) bears a similarly broad connotation.

What "the peace of Torah" (Sifre Num. 42) means, I do not know.

4. *Sifre Deuteronomy.* The reference to "Torah going forth from Jerusalem" (Sifre Deut. 152) surely refers to an encompassing model of life, not merely a legal decision. But, in context a narrow construction may be sustained. If a person "does Torah" and so "did the will of his Father in Heaven" (Sifre Deut. 306), he enjoys the status of a creature from above. If not, he has the status of a creature from below. Israel was disgraced for not becoming wise in "words of Torah"

(Sifre Deut. 309), surely a matter of character, not mere learning. Failure in that respect made it possible for foreigners to rule Israel (Sifre Deut. 45, 323), or for Israel to turn to idolatry (Sifre Deut. 43). "When Israel does the Torah" (Sifre Deut. 5, 40, 319) encompasses fulfilling all its teachings. "Separating [oneself] from the Torah" (Sifre Deut. 43) means the opposite and leads to idolatry. Israel must keep the Torah and ensure that coming generations do so too (Sifre Deut. 335). Jacob kept the whole Torah (Sifre Deut. 336). Whoever rejects idolatry affirms the entire Torah (Sifre Deut. 54)—revelation and its contents. The Torah is the inheritance of Israel (Sifre Deut. 345). "David acted not in accordance with the Torah" (Sifre Deut. 51)—in a particular way, however, not in general.

With the sole qualification concerning the Mekhilta stated earlier, I find it difficult to locate in any of the so-called tannaitic collections of midrashim the conception of the Torah as a source of personal or national salvation. While, to be sure, we may readily move from what these collections do affirm to the natural conclusion that the Torah has the power to save Israel, we cannot conclude that the framers of these collections themselves took that step. For I find few statements that compare to the elaborate corpus of stories found in the Yerushalmi, about sages' power, achieved through the Torah, to afford protection and salvation, or about how the Torah protects Israel in material and concrete ways. The documents just now surveyed scarcely present a counterpart to those convictions that form the Yerushalmi's definitive and (I think) distinctive conception concerning the word Torah. That judgment will take on still greater authority when we see what a collection of midrashim, falling within the framework of the positions outlined in the Talmud of the Land of Israel, has to say about Torah and salvation.

THE SECOND SEQUENCE:
TWO FURTHER VERSE-BY-VERSE
EXEGETICAL COMPOSITIONS.
IN THE NAME OF
LATER AUTHORITIES (AMORAIM).
GENESIS RABBAH AND LEVITICUS RABBAH

The two compilations of exegesis at hand have in common their equal use of two distinct sorts of units of discourse. One type is the verse-by-verse reading of a passage, with some sort of comment, whether citation of a verse in some other book of the Hebrew Scriptures, or a secondary expansion, or an appended statement of another kind. The other type of construction proves more philosophical and discursive. It pursues a theme, citing many verses from diverse passages deemed to intersect with the topic under analysis.

The date of the compilation, or closing, of the documents at hand is difficult to ascertain. Since the two types of units of discourse used here correspond to those we find in the Talmud of the Land of Israel, and since a fair amount of material is shared with that Talmud, it may be that the work of closure occurred at much the same time as did that on the Talmud of the Land of Israel, hence ca. 400 C.E. But that is only a guess.

A still more difficult problem affecting these documents requires specification. Exactly what do we mean when we speak of Genesis Rabbah, Leviticus Rabbah, or any of the subsequent compositions? It is difficult to answer this question. The reason is that the compositions are composites of diverse materials, some particular to a given collection, some shared with other compositions. If we eliminate units of discourse that occur in more than a single collection, e.g., in one of the Talmuds, or in the Tosefta (the Mishnah, for its part, shares nothing, though it may be cited explicitly), there still remains a conglomerate of diverse units of discourse. But to date, the types of units, differentiated by form and literary traits, have not been subjected to systematic classification and sustained description.

My own sense concerning both of the compositions at hand, as well as the group to follow, is that they unite several different strata of materials, each with its distinctive literary preferences and possibly also its favored authorities and viewpoints. So when we speak of the Rabbah-compositions, treating these as unitary documents with characteristic viewpoints expressed throughout the whole of one document (but not expressed in some other document, or not in exactly the same way), we do so for one reason only. The systematic work of differentiation and description remains to be done.

For all these reasons, the work at hand provides only a primitive and preliminary suggestion, nothing more than an overview of an undifferentiated landscape, viewed from a great distance. Happily, as we shall now see, the sole point of importance, fresh and new, emerges in the philosophical conception of the Torah as a blueprint for creation, expressed in the opening passages of Genesis Rabbah (reviewed below). Otherwise, "the Torah" and "Torah" occur in apparently conventional and familiar ways. So while a vast enterprise of literary and conceptual analysis awaits, the preliminary result may prove useful for our larger inquiry. The absence of more refined modes of analysis of the layers or components of the documents at hand constitutes no formidable obstacle to our modest survey.

THE TORAH AS A PARTICULAR THING

1. *Genesis Rabbah.* Gen. R. 9:5 refers to a copy of the Torah belonging to Meir. Meir found no Torah so he recited the contents from memory (Gen. R. 36:8). Among references to a Torah-scroll is Gen. R. 91:3.

2. *Leviticus Rabbah.* This contains many references to matters written in the Torah (e.g., Lev. R. 7:3). I see no reason to give numerous examples of an established usage.

THE TORAH AS REVELATION

1. *Genesis Rabbah.* The systematic exegesis of verses of Scripture in context offers the best evidence that the Torah in these documents, as in all others, constitutes divine revelation. Still, the exegetes who treat the five occurrences of "light" in Genesis 1 as corresponding to the five books of the Pentateuch embellish the notion that the Torah stands for and is called light (Gen. R. 3:5). "The Torah, lights in heaven, and rain" were given as gifts to the world (Gen. R. 6:5). When Adam foresaw that Israel would accept the Torah, he was reconciled to producing descendants (Gen. R. 21:9). The Torah teaches practical wisdom as well (Gen. R. 31:11). The righteous, who accepted the Torah, enjoyed God's favor and reached the mountains of God; the wicked, who rejected it, did not (Gen. R. 33:1).

2. *Leviticus Rabbah.* The warnings of the Torah save Israel from Gehenna (Lev. R. 2:9). The two things held in God's right hand are the Torah and righteousness (Lev. R. 4:1). The Torah provided all sorts of rules and laws (e.g., Lev. R. 10:6). "Wisdom has built her house" (Prov. 9:1) refers to the Torah (Gen. R. 11:3). Various passages invoke proof-texts of Torah, Prophets, and Writings—all meaning revelation (e.g., Lev. R. 16:4). God used circumlocutions in composing the Torah (Lev. R. 26:1).

TORAH AS A PARTICULAR ACT.
AS GENERIC

1. *Genesis Rabbah*. One should sleep a little but labor much in the study of Torah (Gen. R. 9:6). Torah is without measure (Gen. R. 10:1), possibly meaning study of Torah. The reward of study of Torah is a comfortable life (Gen. R. 11:4).

2. *Leviticus Rabbah*. A thousand begin to study Scripture, a hundred go on to the Mishnah, ten proceed to the Talmud, and of these, one gives legal decisions (Lev. R. 2:1). This statement indicates a theory of the curriculum of study, leading to the heights of judicial power. Study of Torah turns people away from iniquity (Lev. R. 3:6). One example of Torah meaning study of Torah identifies the poor man as one poor in knowledge of the Torah (Lev. R. 34:4 on Prov. 29:13).

No examples of the use of the word Torah as generic seem to occur in either compilation.

TORAH AS INDICATOR OF STATUS

1. *Genesis Rabbah*. The distinction between teachings of Torah and teachings of scribes may be implicit at Gen. R. 60:8, which states that the uncleanness of a reptile is based on an explicit statement of the Torah, while the uncleanness of its blood is merely derivative. The status of Torah accorded to persons, places and things, and applied to relationships, does not seem to come under sustained discussion in this compilation. But it is surely implied in the many passages that express high regard for sages, rabbis, study of Torah, and the like.

2. *Leviticus Rabbah*. I find no relevant passages here.

WRITTEN AND ORAL TORAH

1. *Genesis Rabbah*. I find no relevant passages.

2. *Leviticus Rabbah*. One should study Torah, Prophets, Writings, Oral Law, Midrash, and so forth (Lev. R. 3:7). Teachers of Scripture and of the Oral Law "set right the way" (Lev. R. 9:2). Words of Torah were given in clear divisions—Scripture, Mishnah, Talmud, law, and lore (Lev. R. 15:2). This statement seems to me decisive evidence of

the notion that Torah encompasses more than Scripture. There are specialists, of equal merit, in Scripture, Mishnah, Talmud, and lore (Lev. R. 36:2), but the myth of the two Torahs in particular is not attested here.

TORAH AS A WAY OF LIFE

1. *Genesis Rabbah*. Sages would go to hear expositions of the Torah or give them (Gen. R. 35:3). Perhaps associating the Torah with "the land that was pleasant" (Gen. R. 98:12) refers to the way of life of learning.

2. *Leviticus Rabbah*. The Torah served to fence Israel off from the nations (Lev. R. 1:10). By keeping its rules, Israel remains distinct. Israel should both study Torah and also practice good deeds (Lev. R. 3:7). The reward of martyrdom for studying Torah is eternal life (Lev. R. 3:7). One who does not engage in Torah-study engages in empty conversation (Lev. R. 12:1). One of the marks of great Torah-learning is humility (Lev. R. 36:2).

I can point to no passage in Genesis Rabbah or Leviticus Rabbah that clearly portrays the Torah as a source of salvation for Israel or for the individual Jew. What was said above about the so-called tannaitic collections of midrashim applies here too.

THE THIRD SEQUENCE:
COMPILATIONS OF
DISCURSIVE EXPOSITIONS OF THEMES:
LAMENTATIONS RABBAH,
ESTHER RABBAH I,
SONG OF SONGS RABBAH,
RUTH RABBAH, PESIQTA DE RAB KAHANA

The compilations reviewed here appear to come later than those above, but that is no more than an impression and a conventional viewpoint. It is hard to establish what statements testify to the age in which the composition reached closure, and what statements speak of some earlier time. The collections at hand make ample use of materials that occur also in other compilations, some of them certainly earlier. This suggests that the framers of the several documents began with an overall plan of the topics they wished to treat and then did three things. First, they gathered available materials. Second, they revised some of what they had in hand to make it serve their own purpose. Third, they invented new discourses in order to meet the topical requirements of the original plan. This thesis would account for the indiscriminate use of elsewhere attested and unattested units of discourse. For Pesiqta de R. Kahana, moreover, a clearcut plan of treating a topic governs the formation of every Pisqa, as Braude and Kapstein demonstrate. The proems of the other exegetical compilations likewise propose systematically to unpack an announced topic. In this regard the compositions at hand seem more coherent as thematic discussions than those in the earlier group. But, as I said, these are at best impressions. In the aggregate, if we place the materials in the fifth and sixth centuries, we are not apt to err by very much.

THE TORAH AS A PARTICULAR THING

1. *Lamentations Rabbah.* "Reading in the Torah" occurs throughout, as expected, e.g., Proem 11. In this and the following compilations, ample evidence that the Torah is a concrete thing, a scroll, appears throughout. We may simply stipulate this usage at the outset in the other collections under study.

THE TORAH AS REVELATION

1. *Lamentations Rabbah.* Implicit in the systematic exegesis of verses of Lamentations is the conviction that they derive from God's revealed truth. This same fundamental conviction characterizes all the other compilations.

3. *Song of Songs Rabbah.* God says to Israel, "I will give you my Torah, but bring me sureties that you will keep it" (Song R. 1:4:1). The diverse passages of the Torah fit together like pearls (Song R. 1:10:3). People were liable for violating the Torah's rules not when it was revealed, but only after it had been explained (Song R. 2:3:4). The Torah provided an atonement for slander and murder (Song R. 4:4:5).

5. *Pesiqta de R. Kahana.* God prevented the nations from accepting the Torah (5:2) when he revealed it. The Torah gives good advice to

farmers (10:7). The Torah was given fifty days after the Exodus (12:4). It came in three parts (12:13).

TORAH AS A PARTICULAR ACT.
AS GENERIC

1. *Lamentations Rabbah.* Study of Torah gains a wholly salvific sense in this composition. The sages of Israel expounded the Torah chapter by chapter for Nebuchadnezzar (Lam. R. 2:10:14). King David got up early to study the Torah (Lam. R. 2:19:22). The generic usage proves irrelevant; it is simply not applicable to the material.

3. *Song of Songs Rabbah.* One may master Torah-teachings by means of parable (Song R. 1:1:8). Teachers of Torah are Israel's ornaments (Song R. 1:10:2). When one discourses on the Torah in public, he should try to please his audience (Song R. 4:11:1). One should study little by little, but systematically, as in the following passage:

Song of Rabbah 5:11:2
[Translated by M. Simon, pp. 240–41]

R. Yohanan of Sepphoris explained the verse by a parable from heaps (*telulioth*) of dust. A stupid person will say, 'Who can clear away all this?' But a sensible man will say: 'I will clear away two basketfuls by day and two by night, until it is all cleared away.' So a stupid student says: 'Who can learn the whole of the Torah—Nezikin, thirty sections, Kelim, thirty sections?' But the wise student says: 'I will learn two *halachoth* to-day and two to-morrow, until I have learnt the whole.' R. Jannai said: *Wisdom is unattainable to the fool* (Prov. 24:7). It is like a perforated loaf suspended in a room. The fool says, 'Who can bring it down?' But the clever man says: 'Did not someone hang it up there? I will bring two sticks and tie them together and so bring it down.' So the fool says: 'Who can acquire the learning which is in the mind of my teacher?' But the clever one says: 'Did he not learn it from someone else? I will learn two *halachoth* to-day and two to-morrow until I acquire the whole of the learning of this Sage.' R. Levi said: Learning is like a perforated basket the owner of which hired workers to fill it with water. Said the stupid one: 'What good do I do by filling at this end when it flows out at the other?' But the clever one said: 'Do I not get paid for it? Do I not get paid by the owner for every cask?' So the stupid one says: 'If I learn Torah, I forget it; what good do I do?' But the clever one says: 'Does not the Holy One, blessed be He, give me a reward for my labour?'

The reward of studying Torah in this world is to study in the next (Song R. 6:2:6). The houses of study and the children who study Torah are Israel's ornaments (Song R. 6:11:11).

5. *Pesiqta de R. Kahana.* Abner and Amasa were like lions in their understanding of the Torah (4:2). When people study Torah, the words seem fresh (12:21). Torah-teaching is described as follows:

Pesiqta de R. Kahana 12:25
[Translated by Braude and Kapstein, p. 249]

Another comment on *I am the Lord thy God.* R. Hanina bar Papa said: The Holy One appeared to Israel with a stern face, with an equanimous face, with a friendly face, with a joyous face: with a severe face appropriate for the teaching of Scripture—when a man teaches Torah to his son, he must impress upon him his own awe of Torah; with an equanimous face appropriate for the teaching of Mishnah; with a friendly face appropriate for the teaching of Talmud; with a joyous face appropriate for the teaching of 'Agadah. Therefore the Holy One said to them: Though you see Me in all these guises, [I am still One]—*I am the Lord thy God.*

TORAH AS INDICATOR OF STATUS

1. *Lamentations Rabbah.* The distinction between teachings of Torah and teachings of scribes does not occur, apparently because it is not relevant. It evidently serves for legal exegesis only. The same applies to the other four collections.

1. *Lamentations Rabbah.* The status of Torah accorded to persons, places and things, or applied to relationships, plays no explicit role in this compilation. But it surely is implicit in all that is said, e.g., about Torah as a source of salvation. The same applies to the remaining collections.

WRITTEN AND ORAL TORAH

1. *Lamentations Rabbah.* The distinction between Scripture-study, which is for children, and Mishnah-study, for adults, proves common-

place, e.g., Lam. R. Proem 12. The issue of the two forms of the To-rah makes an appearance, e.g., at Proem 1: Israel rejected both Torahs.

2. *Esther Rabbah I*. The usage does not occur.

3. *Song of Songs Rabbah*. Song R. 1:3:2 explicitly refers to the two Torahs, one written, one oral. The distinction between Scripture and Mishnah is implicit in the view that they form counterparts to one an-other (Song R. 1:10:2). A man who has everything knows Scripture, Mishnah, Talmud, Tosefta, and lore (Song R. 1:14:2, cf. 5:13:1).

4. *Ruth Rabbah*. The usage does not occur.

5. *Pesiqta de R. Kahana*. The Mishnah is cited as a decree of God (4:1). Song 5:2 is taken to refer to the written and the oral Torah (5:6). There are numerous other citations of passages of the Mishnah, e.g., 9:3. These are subjected to the same exegetical procedures as apply throughout to verses of Scripture. Other passages that allude to the written and oral Torahs include 10:5, 27:2 (five kinds of joy means Scripture, Mishnah, Talmud, Tosefta, and lore).

TORAH AS A WAY OF LIFE

1. *Lamentations Rabbah*. I find no passages demanding classifica-tion here. But at numerous points a life of obedience to the Torah —not merely study of it—constitutes the highest value.

2. *Esther Rabbah I*. The usage does not occur.

3. *Song of Songs Rabbah*. The following passage captures the am-ple dimensions of Torah as a way of conducting life and attaining salvation:

Song of Songs Rabbah 1:2:3
[Translated by M. Simon, pp. 33–36]

For thy loved ones are better than wine. The words of the Torah are compared to water, to wine, to oil, to honey, and to milk.

To water: *Ho, everyone that thirsteth come ye for water* (Is. 55:1).

Just as water stretches from one end of the world to the other, as it says, *To him that spread forth the earth above the waters* (Ps. 136:6), so the Torah goes from one end of the world to the other, as it says, *The measure thereof is longer than the earth* (Job 11:9).

Just as water is a source of life for the world, as it says, *A fountain of gardens, a well of living waters* (S.S. 4:15), so the Torah is a source of life for the world, as it says, *For they are life unto those that find them and health to all their flesh* (Prov. 4:22); and it is also written, *Come ye, buy and eat* (Is. 55:1).

Just as water is from heaven, as it says, *At the sound of His giving a multitude of waters in the heavens* (Jer. 10:13), so the Torah is from heaven, as it says, *I have talked with you from heaven* (Ex. 20:19). Just as [the downpour of] water is accompanied by loud thunderings, as it says, *The voice of the Lord is upon the waters* (Ps. 29:3), so the Torah was given with loud thunderings, as it says, *And it came to pass on the third day when it was morning that there were thunders and lightnings* (Ex. 19:16).

Just as water restores the soul, as it says, *But God cleaved the hollow place which was in Lehi and there came water thereout; and when he had drunk . . . he revived* (Judg. 15:19), so does the Torah, as it says, *The law of the Lord is perfect, restoring the soul* (Ps. 19:8).

Just as water purifies man from ritual uncleanness, as it says, *And I will sprinkle clean water upon you, and ye shall be clean* (Ez. 36:25), so the Torah cleanses an unclean man of his uncleanness, as it says, *The words of the Lord are pure words* (Ps. 12:7).

Just as water cleanses the body, as it says, *He shall bathe himself in water* (Lev. 17:15), so the Torah cleanses the body, as it says, *Thy word is purifying to the uttermost* (Ps. 119:140).

Just as water covers the nakedness of the sea, as it says, *As the waters cover the sea* (Is. 11:9), so the Torah covers the nakedness of Israel, as it says, *Love covereth all transgressions* (Prov. 10:12).

Just as rain water comes down in drops and forms rivers, so with the Torah; a man learns two *halachahs* to-day and two to-morrow, until he becomes like a flowing stream. Just as water has no taste unless one is thirsty, so the Torah has no taste unless one labours at it.

Just as water leaves a high place and flows to a low one, so the Torah leaves one whose spirit is proud and cleaves to one whose spirit is lowly.

Just as water does not keep well in a vessel of silver or gold but in the commonest of vessels, so the Torah resides only in one who makes himself like a vessel of earthenware.

Just as with water a great man is not ashamed to say to a lowly man, 'Give me a drink of water,' so with the words of the Torah, a great scholar must not be ashamed to say to a lesser one, 'Teach me one chapter, or one statement, or one verse, or even one letter.'

Just as with water, if one does not know how to swim in it, he will be drowned, so with the words of the Torah, if one does not know how to thread his way in them and to instruct in accordance with them, he will ultimately come to grief.

Said R. Hanina of Caesarea: Seeing that water is conducted not only to gardens and orchards, but also to baths and privies, am I to say that it is the same with the words of the Torah? Not so, since it says, *For the ways of the Lord are right* (Hos. 14:10).

R. Hama b. Ukba said: Just as water makes plants grow, so the words of the Torah nurture everyone who labours over them as they require.

Shall I say that just as water becomes stale and noisome in the jar, so the words of the Torah? Not so, since it says, that it is like wine: just as, the longer wine matures in the jar the better it becomes, so the more the words of the Torah become ingrained in a man, the greater the reputation they win for him.

Shall I say that just as water after being drunk is imperceptible in the body, so are the words of the Torah? Not so, since it is compared with wine: just as wine leaves its mark when drunk, so words of Torah leave their mark, and people point with the finger and say, that is a scholar.

Shall I say that just as water does not gladden the heart, so the words of the Torah? Not so, since it is compared with wine: just as wine rejoices the heart, as it is written, *And wine that maketh glad the heart of man* (Ps. 104:15), so words of Torah rejoice the heart, as it says, *The precepts of the Lord are right, rejoicing the heart* (Ps. 19:9).

Shall I say that just as wine is sometimes bad for the head and the body, so are the words of the Torah also? Not so, since it is compared to oil: just as oil makes the head and the body feel pleasant, so the words of the Torah make the head and the body feel pleasant, as it says, *Thy word is a lamp unto my feet* (Ps. 119:105).

Shall I say then that just as oil is bitter at first and sweet afterwards, so are the words of the Torah? Not so, since it is compared to milk and honey: just as these are sweet throughout, so are the words of the Torah, as it says, *Sweeter also than honey* (ib. 19:11).

Shall I say that just as honey has wax-cells, so also the words of the Torah? Not so, since it is compared to milk: just as milk is pure, so are the words of the Torah pure, as it says, *Gold and glass cannot equal it* (Job 28:17). Shall I say that just as milk is insipid, so are the words of the Torah? Not so, since it is compared to milk and honey: just as milk and honey when combined do not injure the body, so the words of the Torah, as it says, *It shall be health to thy navel* (Prov. 3:8), and, *For they are life unto those that find them* (ib. 4:22).

Because of its comprehensive character, this passage serves as the summa of the thought of formative Judaism about the critical image and symbol of that system. Let us therefore take a moment to categorize the usages of the word Torah in this remarkable construction.

First and foremost, we see that the word Torah proves much more encompassing than merely a scroll or its contents. It serves here as a way of referring to the entire doctrine we now call "Judaism." Thus the Torah "spreads over the entire world" (whatever that means); it is a source of life; it restores the soul; it cleanses an unclean man of his uncleanness; it covers the nakedness of Israel. All of these richly metaphorical statements evoke through the word Torah the conviction that Israel defines itself, finds life, is saved, by "the Torah." The contrast to the next group of metaphors shows us how distinctive is the first usage. For when the framers of the passage wish to speak of the Torah as something one learns, they are perfectly able to come down to earth and produce concrete and finite statements. So a person must work hard to study Torah; he must be humble in studying the Torah; he must be willing to admit his ignorance; he must have a teacher. The more familiar usages of the Mishnaic sector of the canon—Torah as a source of revelation, Torah as a way of life—likewise occur. So, in all, the passage at hand provides a summary and prospectus of all of the rich meanings imputed to the word Torah at the climax and conclusion of the formative centuries of Judaism.

One should sell all his possessions for the sake of studying Torah (Song R. 8:7:1).

4. *Ruth Rabbah.* A father may dedicate his son to a life of Torah-study (Ruth R. 6:4).

5. *Pesiqta de R. Kahana.* Abbahu lit up when he learned a passage of the Tosefta (4:4). The reward of faithful tithing is a long life of study of Torah (10:2). Those who earn a living should give a tithe of their earnings to support those who study Torah (10:10). Torah is found among those who do acts of mercy (12:8). When David sought counsel, he looked into the Torah (12:12). Torah is at its best when it comes from the mouths of old men (12:24). Teachers must be supported (27:1).

TORAH AS A SOURCE OF SALVATION

1. *Genesis Rabbah.* When, at Gen. R. 1:1, we find, "God looked into the Torah and created the world," we deal with a conception of the Torah that transcends the category of revelation. Now Torah stands for the blueprint of creation itself. It follows (Gen. R. 1:4; 8:2) that the Torah was created before the world, and, as Banaiah says

(Gen. R. 1:4; 8:2), "The world and the fullness thereof were created only for the sake of the Torah." This conception places the Torah into the grid of nature and supernature, rather than of Israel's history and destiny. Accordingly, here Torah stands for something other than salvation. But so far as the sage masters the secrets of creation through his knowledge of the Torah, I suppose he can serve to save Israel. So, by extension, we may not totally err in classifying the cited statements as we have. It is clear, however, that here the Torah has left all concrete categories behind, becoming an adumbration of heavenly wisdom (Gen. R. 44:17).

We take note, therefore, that the word Torah now represents a conception quite remote from its original meaning as a scroll and its contents. The contents, the way of life scarcely relate to this far deeper, more abstract, philosophical conception. The Torah here is read as God's plan or design for the world, the medium for the message of creation. Now that conception of the Torah, deeply metaphysical, possibly mystical, as it is, carries us far from the usages of the word familiar in the Mishnaic sector of the rabbinic canon. We cannot claim that this extreme abstract symbolization of the word Torah necessarily conveys the message of the Torah as a source of salvation. Yet I can point to no other passsage, within the entire canon of formative Judaism, at which the Torah appears in so otherworldly a guise. Clearly, the framers of Genesis Rabbah imagine that the Torah preserves the metaphysical mysteries and defines the ground plan of all being, natural and supernatural alike. That conception occurs in more than one unit of thought. It underlies a range of discussions. Accordingly, a fresh and original kind of thought stands behind the inaugural units of this compilation. For that mode of thought, the word Torah bears a range of meanings otherwise difficult to attest. On that account we posit a range of reflection on the word Torah at best tangential to, perhaps intersecting with, that of the framers of the rest of the canon, early and late. More than this we cannot say on the basis of the modest survey at hand.

2. *Leviticus Rabbah.* The exiles will be gathered in because of the merit of the study of Mishnah (Lev. R. 7:3). When Israel studies the Mishnah, it is as if they offer sacrifices. The high priest had the merit of Torah, among his other merits, when he entered the holy of holies (Lev. R. 21:6). "The path of life" (Prov. 15:24) refers to the Torah (Lev. R. 29:5). All these statements address the issue of salvation.

3. *Lamentations Rabbah.* Keeping and studying the Torah preserves the city, while failure to do so destroys it, as in the following passage of fundamental importance:

Lamentations Rabbah Proem 2

[Translated by A. Cohen, pp. 2–4]

R. Abba b. Kahana opened his discourse with the text, *Who is the wise man, that he may understand this?* (Jer. 9:11). R. Simeon b. Yohai taught: If you behold cities uprooted from their site in the land of Israel, know that the inhabitants failed to pay the fees of the instructors in Bible and Mishnah; as it is said, *Wherefore is the land perished? . . . And the Lord saith: Because they have forsaken My law* (ib. 11 f.).

Rabbi sent R. Assi and R. Ammi on a mission to organise [religious education in] the cities of the land of Israel. They came to a city and said to the people, 'Bring us the guardians of the city.' They fetched the captain of the guard and the magistrate. The Rabbis exclaimed, 'These the guardians of the city! They are its destroyers!' The people inquired, 'Who, then, are its guardians?' and they answered, 'The instructors in Bible and Mishnah, who meditate upon, teach and preserve the Torah day and night.' This is in accordance with what is said, *Thou shalt meditate therein day and night* (Josh. 1:8); and it is similarly stated, *Except the Lord build the house, they labour in vain that build it* (Ps. 127:1).

R. Huna and R. Jeremiah said in the name of R. Samuel b. R. Isaac: We find that the Holy One, blessed be He, may overlook idolatry, immorality, or bloodshed, but He does not overlook rejection of the Torah; as it is said, —'*Wherefore is the land perished?*' It is not written here 'because of idolatry, immorality, or bloodshed,' but '*because they have forsaken My law.*'

R. Huna and R. Jeremiah said in the name of R. Hiyya b. Abba: It is written, *They have forsaken Me and have not kept My law* (Jer. 16:11)—i.e., would that they had forsaken Me but kept My law, since by occupying themselves therewith, the light which it contains would have led them back to the right path . . . .

Samuel taught in the name of R. Samuel b. Ammi: When can the Government enact an oppressive measure and render it effective? At the time that Israel casts words of Torah to the ground; and so it is written, *And the host was given over to it together with the continual burnt-offering through transgression* (Dan. 8:12). 'Host' signifies nothing else than the [non-Jewish] Governments; as it is said, *The Lord will punish the host of the high heaven on high* (Is. 24:21). —'*The continual burnt-offering*' is Israel; as it is written, '*Thou shalt meditate therein day and night.*' '*Through transgression*' means through neglect of Torah. Whenever Israel casts words of Torah to the ground, the Government enacts an oppressive measure which proves effective, as it is said, *And it cast down truth to the ground* (Dan. *ib.*). '*Truth*' signifies nothing else than Torah; as it is said, *Buy the truth, and sell it not* (Prov. 23:23). If you have cast words of Torah to the ground, the Government is immediately successful [in its oppressive measures]; and so it is written, *And it wrought, and prospered* (Dan. *ib.*).

R. Judah b. Pazzi said: *Israel hath cast off that which is good* (Hos. 8:3). '*Good*' signifies nothing else than Torah; as it is said, *For I give you good doctrine* (Prov. 4:2).

R. Abba b. Kahana said: There arose not among the heathen peoples philosophers like Balaam the son of Beor and Oenamos of Gadara. They were once asked, 'Can we overcome this people [of Israel]'? They replied, 'Go round to their Synagogues; if there is a hum of children's voices [there studying the Torah], you cannot prevail over them, otherwise you can. For thus their patriarch assured them, saying, "*The voice is the voice of Jacob, but the hands are the hands of Esau*" (Gen. 27:22)—i.e., so long as the voice of Jacob persists in the Synagogues and Houses of Study, the hands are not Esau's hands; but whenever there is no hum of voices in the Synagogues and Houses of Study, the hands are Esau's hands.' Similarly it declares, *Therefore as stubble devoureth the tongue of fire* (Is. 5:24). Can stubble devour fire? Is it not the nature of fire to devour stubble, and yet you say '*As stubble devoureth the tongue of fire*'! In fact, '*stubble*' denotes the house of Esau; as it is said, *And the house of Jacob shall be a fire, and the house of Joseph a flame, and the house of Esau for stubble* (Obad. 18). '*The tongue of fire*' denotes the house of Jacob. '*And as the chaff is consumed in the flame*' (Is. *ib.*) denotes the house of Joseph. '*So their root shall be as rottenness*' (*ib.*) denotes the patriarchs who are the roots of Israel. '*And their blossom shall go up as dust*' denotes the tribes who are the blossoms of Israel. Why [will this fate befall them]? '*Because they have rejected the law of the Lord of hosts*' (*ib.*). R. Judan said: '*Because they have rejected the law of the Lord of hosts*' denotes the written Torah; '*and contemned the word of the Holy One of Israel*' (*ib.*) denotes the oral Torah. Since they cast the words of Torah to the ground, Jeremiah began to lament over them, *Ekah*.

The same viewpoint recurs at Proems 7 and 8. Because he subsisted on little and taught much, Sadoq could save Jerusalem (Lam. R. 1:5:31). The Torah kept Israel from perishing (Lam. R. 3:21:7). Keeping and studying the Torah saves Israel in its dispersion.

The authors of the two Talmuds would not have been surprised by a single assertion in this passage; many of the units of the composition occur also in one or another of those documents. Towns are destroyed through neglect of teachers of the Torah. Towns are preserved by the achievements of masters of the Torah. God forgives anything but neglect of the Torah. Torah-learning will redeem Israel. The government can succeed in oppressing Israel only when Israel rejects the Torah. Israel endures when children repeat Torah-traditions aloud. The entire repertoire of specific statements that express the view of the Torah as a source of salvation finds illustration in this passage. It comprises nothing less than a composite article on that very subject. So we find the following apologetic for Israel:

Lamentations Rabbah 3:66:9
[Cohen, pp. 12, 13]

R. Eliezer says: Because Amalek sought to destroy Israel from beneath the wings of heaven, Moses spake before the Holy One, blessed be He: 'This wicked one has come to destroy Israel from beneath Thy wings, so who will read in Thy Torah which Thou hast given them?'

The fundamental principle is that the Torah saves Israel from the kingdoms, and neglect of Torah subjugates Israel to them. So the Torah constitutes Israel's salvation and governs Israel's fate.

5. *Song of Songs Rabbah.* Whoever discourses on the Torah in public merits that His Holy Spirit rest on him (Song R. 1:1:82; cf. 1:2:5). Words of Torah are like a weapon (Song R. 1:2:5). They confer life in this world and in the world to come. The elaborate passage of Song R. 1:2:3, cited above, contains a still more extensive account of the power of the Torah to effect salvation. Because Israel neglects to study Torah and keep the commandments, it suffers a long night of oppression (Song R. 3:1:1). The Jew who studies the Torah in this world will continue to do so in the world to come (Song R. 6:2:6). The Torah pleads in behalf of Israel.

6. *Ruth Rabbah.* If Israel had not accepted the Torah, the world would have reverted to desolation (Ruth R. Proem 1). Israel would have disappeared (Ruth R. Proem 1).

7. *Pesiqta de R. Kahana.* The words of Torah stand up for him who works to understand them (12:5). If Israel obeys the Torah, God will speak in their defense (12:23). God punishes Israel for neglect of

study of Torah. But when Israel studies Torah, they are saved from their enemies.

The Torah is what sustains Israel in its long exile and will bring its reward at the end. Because Israel does not consume enough bread of Torah, Israel has to perform forced labor (27:1).

Pesiqta de R. Kahana 19:4

[Translated by Braude and Kapstein, pp. 326–27]

R. Abba bar Kahana, citing R. Yohanan, taught in a parable: A king who wed a noblewoman wrote out a pledge of a substantial settlement upon her: "Such-and-such elegant chambers, canopied over, I will provide for you. Such-and-such ornaments I will give you. Such-and-such treasures I will give you." Then he left her and went away to a far country by the sea where he remained many years. Eventually her companions began to mock her, saying: "How much longer will you wait around here? Get yourself a man while you are young and while your strength is with you." Thereupon she would go into her house, pick up her marriage settlement, read it, and be comforted. After many years, the king came back from the far country by the sea. He said to his wife: "My little one, I marvel that you could wait around for me all these years." She replied: "My lord the king, but for the substantial marriage settlement which you pledged to me in writing, my companions would long since have got me to give you up."

[As her companions mocked the king's wife], so, the world being what it is, the nations of the earth mock Israel and say to them: How long will you sacrifice yourselves for your God, giving up your lives for Him, letting yourselves be slain for His sake? How much pain He has brought upon you! How many plunderers He has brought upon you! How many afflictions He has brought upon you! Get yourselves over to us, and we shall make you captains, prefects, and commanders-in-chief! Israel's reply to the nations is to go into synagogues and into houses of study, take the Scroll, and read in it God's pledges to her: *I will have respect unto you, and make you fruitful, and multiply you; and will establish My covenant with you* (Lev. 26:9). And thus Israel comforts herself.

When the time of redemption arrives, the Holy One will say to Israel: "I marvel that you were able to wait for Me all these years," and Israel will reply to the Holy One: Master of universes, but for the Scroll which Thou didst write for us, the nations of the world would long since have got us to give Thee up. Of the Torah it is written *This*—[as in *This is the Torah* (Deut. 4:44)]—*I recall to my mind, therefore have I hope* (Lam.

3:21). And David said likewise: *Unless Thy Torah had been my delight,
I should then have perished in mine affliction* (Ps. 119:92).

We find in the Pesiqta's powerful parable the ultimate formulation of
the idea at hand, a fresh and original way of expressing what others,
from the Talmud of the Land of Israel onward, had been trying to say.
While we may assume that the authors of the documents of the Mishnaic sector of the canon would have concurred in the basic proposition, we must observe that this usage of the word Torah begins only
within the talmudic part of the canon and undergoes its richest and
most evocative developments there alone.

BETWEEN THE MISHNAH
AND THE TALMUD

This survey yields information on two separate matters. First, we
have seen how the word Torah is used in a category of rabbinical writings distinct from those framed around the Mishnah. The exegetical
compilations are organized as commentaries not to the Mishnah but
to Scripture. They deal, in the main, not with matters of law, but with
matters of biblical lore and theology. This gives us the opportunity to
see whether, when the founders of Judaism in its formative centuries
worked on something other than normative law, they used language
or symbols in some way different from that found suitable for legal
discourse. The answer is that they did not. The familiar uses of the
word Torah recur. All of them are attested in nearly all of the documents at hand. That is the case, even though, as I said, the context of
discourse is so different. If people wish to distinguish documents that
deal with Scripture, or with exegesis and lore in general, they cannot
do so on the basis of the usage of key-words and concepts. A single
language unites both kinds of books. It follows that the established
distinction between one type, "law," from the other, "lore," must
come under review. For it appears, from the present perspective, to
constitute a distinction without a difference.

Second, we discover that we can indeed distinguish among the diverse collections of biblical exegesis, though by an unanticipated criterion. That new point of differentiation emerges from the way in
which ideas collected in a given composition relate to those gathered
in another composition. What emerges is this. Some collections of ex-

egesis use the word Torah only as the Mishnah does; so they fall within the same circle as the Mishnah, along with its closely associated documents, Abot and Tosefta. Other collections repeat fresh ideas about the word Torah, which we already have found in the Talmud of the Land of Israel and shall see in abundance in the Talmud of Babylonia.

At the same time, there is a negative result to be specified, as suggested just now. We cannot distinguish within the rabbinic canon by reference to whether a document contains legal, as distinct from nonlegal (theological-exegetical) materials. We sort out documents, rather not on the basis of law as against lore, but by reference to their close relationship to the Mishnah's ideas, on the one hand, or to those of the Talmuds, on the other. Some collections of exegesis fall within the Mishnah's frame of reference, others within that of the Talmud. That is precisely what we find when we examine the provenance of ideas about the Messiah in the various documents of the rabbinic canon, as we saw in *Messiah in Context*.

The exegetical collections that present pretty much the same ideas as the Mishnah are conventionally called tannaitic, because the names of most authorities ("tannas" or repeaters of sayings) cited in them occur also in the Mishnah. Whether or not the documents themselves derive from the second century, or make pseudepigraphic use of the names of Mishnah's sages, or contain traditions deriving originally from the second century but written down only later, we cannot now say. To call the Mekhilta, the Sifra, and the two Sifres "tannaitic" is certainly correct from the viewpoint of the present results. Whether opinions in the documents derive from actual Tannaim, that is, Mishnah-teachers, we do not know. But the opinions on the issue at hand, that is, on the meaning of "Torah," we find in the Mishnah, and do not cover the range of opinions we find in the two Talmuds.

In the case of other midrash-compilations, by contrast, we find some ideas about the word Torah entirely familiar from and distinctive to the two Talmuds. Pesiqta de R. Kahana, the last surveyed, falls entirely within the frame of meaning established by the Talmuds. So, as I said, we reach a somewhat unexpected result in this survey (as we did in the study of the Messiah in the rabbinic canon), in finding grounds for differentiating among documents of a literature generally believed to constitute a uniform and coherent corpus.

Having differentiated one group of compilations of scriptural exegesis from another, we may now ask of the whole: Just how important is the conception of Torah in the entire mass? The criterion for establishing its importance comes to us from Abot, in which, as we saw in detail, the Torah forms, if not a central category, at least a persistent theme. By that criterion, no compilation within the Mishnaic sector of the canon at hand passes muster. For all of them, the Torah in its conventional, Mishnaic meanings forms part of a scarcely differentiated backdrop. The Torah does not constitute discourse. It is what people do when they speak of other things—that at best. We adduce, by contrast, the amazing notions of Genesis Rabbah, on the one side, and the elaborate statements on the Torah as a source of salvation now reviewed, on the other. Both of these documents fall within the talmudic sector. But for the whole of the Mishnaic sector, by contrast, the Torah symbolizes, more than it says. It defines the range of discourse but does not determine its contents or direction. It is not usually the word authors use to speak of salvation. Obviously, these broad judgments rest on impressions. But the part of this survey based on concordances reinforces the impression that for the documents under study—the so-called tannaitic collections—the word Torah not only is used in just about the same ways that it is used in the Mishnah. It also is no more important or critical a symbol than we find it to be in the Mishnah.

In fact, the Torah emerges as definitive symbol and powerful, evocative abstraction only when the word Torah serves to embody and express the hope for salvation. That is the point at which the word Torah forms the organizing principle for protracted compositions, sustained discourses of remarkable power, such as we have seen both in the Talmud of the Land of Israel and in some of the collections of exegesis associated with its principal ideas and images.

Now when we ask, where have we seen such a result before, the answer, to readers of this trilogy, is obvious. The image of the Messiah as a salvific figure in the foreground of Israel's life, the Messiah as a critical focus of sustained discourse—that image scarcely occurs in the Mishnaic sector of the canon. But it proves ubiquitous in the talmudic sector. For the Mishnah and its cohorts, the Messiah, like the Torah, remains part of the general undifferentiated background. True, people know about the Messiah. But the figure of the Messiah plays no significant part even in discussions of teleology. In the talmudic sector, by contrast, we find numerous references to the Messiah, an entire repertoire of facts and ideas about him, formed into doctrine, that simply play no role in the Mishnaic part of the canon. Important and sustained discussions about the Messiah, when he will come, how he will do his work, and especially, the conditions in which Israel may merit his coming—these occur only in the talmudic, and nowhere in the Mishnaic, sector.

So both the salvific figure of the Messiah and the salvific meaning imputed to the word Torah gain prominence only in the talmudic part of the formative canon. That fact tells us that the framers of the Talmud wished to construct and express a large-scale theory of Israel's salvation. To do so, they turned to enhancing the teleological, and revising the doctrinal, components of their larger inherited system. As I showed in *Messiah in Context*, the rabbinical philosophers reappropriated the entire corpus of available messianic convictions and reshaped a fair part of the whole to accord with the larger principles of their system. They came up with a rabbi-Messiah, who could promise salvation on the terms dictated by the ethos of the rabbis' system of sanctification. We now see how the symbol through which the rabbinic system would express the notion of doctrine—source, justification and validation—is transformed into a salvific symbol, an instrument in a far larger enterprise to portray the means of Israel's salvation. If we then assign the composition of the collections at hand —the two Talmuds and the associated compilations of exegesis—to the fourth, fifth, and sixth centuries, we may justifiably conclude that the age at hand presented Israel with a paramount and urgent question: How long, O Lord—and how? To that question, our sages presented their answer.

6

The Talmud of
Babylonia

ENCYCLOPEDIA AND SUMMA

People generally suppose that the Talmud of Babylonia reached closure at about 500 C.E., but that date is no more than a rough guess. The text remained fluid for a long time to come. Before the ninth century C.E. we have no firm evidence, outside the pages of the Talmud itself, that anyone knew and used the document. The fact is, however, that whenever we date the document, the Talmud at hand stands at the end of the formative period of Judaism. It probably reached closure later than any of the compositions we have surveyed to this point. (The sole exception may prove to be one or two of the compilations of scriptural exegesis.)

The Babylonian Talmud has formed the definitive statement of Judaism from the time of its closure to the present day. This was for good reason. The excellence of its composition, the mastery and authority of those who everywhere studied it and advocated its law, the sharpness of its exegesis and discussion—these secured for the document its paramount position. But I believe there was, yet, a further factor in its success: the comprehensive character of its statement. The Babylonian Talmud incorporates a far broader selection of antecedent materials than any other document that reaches us out of Judaism in late antiquity, far more, for instance, than the Talmud of the Land of Israel. This vast selection, moreover, is so organized and put together that systematic accounts of numerous important problems of biblical exegesis, as well as law and theology emerge. Consequently, the Talmud at hand serves as both an encyclopedia of knowledge and a summa of the theology and law of Judaism.

The present survey will be thorough, because it rests upon Kasovsky's completed concordance for the Talmud of Babylonia. I categorize virtually every usage of the word Torah, listing the vast majority of references. While, for the reader, the result may prove tedious, its solidity repays the tedium. When I claim that the word Torah is used only in the ways I describe, that claim rests upon the incontrovertible evidence of Kasovsky's data as I classify them. Why is it important to know that the word is used in only the specified ways? The answer is, first, that I now demonstrate what I was able to do no more than claim in the preceding two chapters. The word Torah in the talmudic sector of the canon is used in all the ways in which the Mishnaic component uses it, but also in one additional way: Torah as a source of salvation. Second, the Talmud of Babylonia often is misrepresented as disorganized, so beyond all possibility of rational taxonomy. That allegation is simply false.

Why, further, is it important to survey and catalogue the vast majority of occurrences of the word Torah? Only by so doing can we see how the established taxa serve even the enormous number of usages found in the document at hand. That is to say, while the Talmud of Babylonia is far larger in volume and far more diverse in contents than any preceding document, and while, for our purpose, we find an incomparably broader range of discourse featuring the word Torah, the familiar categories of classification continue to serve without substantial revision. Still, I cannot claim that the contents of this chapter will provide such interesting reading as I might wish. With that apology, let us turn to our survey.

THE TORAH AS A PARTICULAR THING

"Torah" as a Torah-scroll, that may be handled, bought, sold, and otherwise disposed of as an object, occurs at b. Ta. 27a; b. B.B. 151a. On certain occasions two or even three scrolls of law are used in synagogue worship, as at b. Yoma 70a; Sot. 41a; Meg. 29b. A king writes two Torahs (b. San. 21a–b). "Reading in the Torah" or other scrolls occurs at b. Meg. 23a and many other passages. One may be guilty of burning a Torah (b. Shab. 115b; Qid. 39b; b. San. 103b). One says a blessing over the Torah, meaning, on the occasion of reading from the Torah (b. Yoma 70a; b. Sot. 41a). Further references to "reading in the Torah" (as distinct from "laboring" or "occupying oneself in/with

Torah"—thus Torah as study—) are as follows: b. Ber. 10b, 22b; Yoma 52a (verses in Scripture), Suk. 41b; R.H. 27a, 32b; Ta. 16a, 27b (= b. Meg. 21a), 30a; Meg. 7a (a verse written in the Torah), 9b, 14a, 21b, 23a, 24a, 25b, 32a; M.Q. 15a, 21a; Sot. 39b; Men. 30a.

Further references to a scroll of the Torah as a physical object appear as follows: b. Ber. 8a, 18a, 25b, 26a, 58a; Shab. 14a (= Meg. 32a), 49b (= b. Qid. 30a), 94b, 115b, 116a (fragments of a scroll of the Torah), 117a, 120a, 133b (= b. Naz. 2b); Er. 64a, 86b (= b. Suk. 16b), 91a; Yoma 70a; Ta. 20a–b (= b. San. 106a), Meg. 21b, 26b–27a, 32a; M.Q. 25a, 26a; Yeb. 16b, 61b, 96b; Ket. 77b; Ned. 25a; Naz. 2b; Sot. 39a–b, 41a; Git. 19b, 45a–b, 52a, 54b, 56b, 60a; Qid. 30a, 33b; B.Q. 17a, 87b; B.M. 29b, 59a; B.B. 14a–b, 15a, 20b, 43a, 52a, 151a; San. 21b (the king writes his own Torah-scroll), 101a, 102b, 106a; Mak. 22b (one rises before a Torah-scroll and also before a great authority), A.Z. 2a, 8b, 18a; Men. 29b, 30a, 32a–b, 42b, 99b; b. Ber. 18a, 23b; Sub. 41a; Shab. 79b, 94b; B.B. 14a, 20a; Meg. 9a; B.B. 43b; Shebu. 38b; Ber. 24a; Shab. 105b (similar to a scroll of the Torah that was burned), 117b; M.Q. 25a; Shab. 116a (scrolls of the Torah); B.B. 14a; San. 68a. At b. Men. 99b, Joshua is promised that the scroll of the Torah will never leave him.

The discourse on whether or not the Torah was given "scroll by scroll" (b. Git. 60a) presupposes revelation of a concrete scroll containing writing. So too the alphabet in which the document was written is specified (b. San. 21b). One may not remove a single letter from the Torah (b. Yeb. 79a). Israel wrote the Torah (b. Sot. 35b, 36b). One may refer to the entire Torah as "a scroll" (b. Sot. 60a). "Writing the words of the Torah in seventy languages" occurs at b. Sot. 36a. People are accused of fraudulently writing their own ideas in a Torah, e.g., "You have counterfeited your Torah" (b. Sot. 30b; San. 90b). The whole of the Torah might have been written on the authority of someone other than Moses (b. Meg. 18b). Joshua wrote a few verses of the Torah (b. B.B. 14b, 15a). These usages presuppose that we speak of a Torah-scroll. The Torah also is hypostatized, as "the Torah dons sackcloth and stands before the Holy One . . ." (b. San. 101a).

"Torah" in the sense of the Pentateuch (as distinguished from Prophets and Writings) occurs at b. R.H. 32a; b. Ta. 8a, 21b, 24a, 27a; b. Ket. 50a; b. B.B. 13b, 14a; b. Meg. 15a (the five-part Torah), b. Ned. 22b; b. San. 44a; b. Hag. 14a; M.Q. 18b; Yoma 69b (Pentateuch vs. Prophetic book), R.H. 32b; Ta. 16a, 30a; Meg. 23a, 24a,

31a; M.Q. 15a, 21a; Sot. 41a; B.Q. 926; San. 101a (study of Torah as distinct from study of prophets). "Oraita" distinguished from "prophets" and "writings"—hence, Pentateuch—occurs at Er. 17a; Qid. 49a. "The Torah of Moses, your rabbi" (b. Meg. 9a, cf. San. 91a) is a document in which writing is found. The Aramaic equivalent occurs at Yoma 36b; b. Yeb. 39b. Written "in oraita," meaning, in the Torah, further appears at Ber. 33b; Mes. 25a, 47b; Shab. 109b; Ta. 9a; Hag. 4b; Ket. 10b, 29b, 56b, 70a; B.Q. 41a; San. 52b, 100b; Shebu. 35a; Zeb. 41a; Hul. 59a; Bek. 40b, 41a, 43a; Pes. 3b.

The text of the Torah was translated into Aramaic (b. Meg. 3a; Shab. 115b).

TORAH AS REVELATION

The Torah as source of revealed truth functions in familiar ways, e.g., prohibiting, permitting, saying, speaking, and the like. The instances of appeal to the contents of Torah as revelation all refer in some way to a verse of Scripture. Passages in which the word Torah refers to authoritative and revealed law are as follows: b. Ber. 25a; b. Shab. 13a, 63a, 119a; b. Er. 13a; b. Pes. 54b; Pes. 119b (the Torah will prohibit . . .), b. Yoma 42b; b. Suk. 5a (the Torah assigned fixed dimensions), b. R.H. 24a–b (= b. A.Z. 43a), b. R.H. 28b; b. Bes. 13b, 25b, 32b; b. Ta. 22b; b. Hag. 10b; b. Yeb. 88b, 117b; Ket. 22b; Sot. 31b, 47b ("the Torah accorded credibility to a witness of a certain status . . ."), b. Yeb. 97a; b. Ket. 32b, 34b, 35a, b, 38a, b, 42b; b. Ned. 4a; b. Naz. 2b; b. Sot. 3a, 4b ("receiving Torah"), b. Sot. 14a ("Torah teaches proper conduct"), b. Git. 42b, 44a ("Torah goes forth . . ."), b. Qid. 21b, 78a; b. B.Q. 26b, 52b (= 53a, 54a), 57a, 60a, 70b, 79b, 87b, 101a; b. B.M. 59b, 61b (= b. B.B. 89b), 69b, 85a, 87a, 91a, 111a; b. B.B. 89b; b. San. 4b, 62b, 64b, 72a, 90a; b. Mak. 13b; b. Shebu. 3b, 21a, 17b; b. A.Z. 17a, 43a, 51a; b. Zeb. 47a, 91a; b. Men. 15b, 84a, 90b, 92b, 93a, 96a–b, 108a–b; b. Bek. 9b, 11a, 13a (Torah has decreed in their regard), b. Tem. 3b; b. Ker. 19b; b. Me. 20a.

Further passages in which we find the phrase, "in the Torah" or "which are in the Torah" meaning "revealed truth" or equivalent are as follows: b. Ber. 11a, 16b (= Suk. 25a, 6b), 14b, 18a (= Suk. 26a; M.Q. 23b), 20b; Shab. 13b, 26b, 31a, 69a, 107a–b; Er. 21a; Pes.

6b, 104a; Yoma 85b (all transgressions noted in the Torah), R.H. 10a;
Meg. 14a (what is written in the Torah), 31a, 32a; M.Q. 23b (commandments written in the Torah), Hag. 2b, 3a; Yeb. 3b, 4b, 63b, 97a;
Ket. 47b, 56b, 83b, 84a (a stipulation contrary to what is written in
the Torah) (= Naz. 11a; Git. 84b; B.M. 94a; Qid. 19b; Mak. 3b);
Ned. 12b, 14a; Naz. 5a; Sot. 37b, 47b; Git. 49b, 57b; Qid. 13b, 29b,
32a, 37b, 39b; B.Q. 34a, 49b, 50a, 87a; B.M. 59a–b; San. 52b,
54a–b, 63b, 66a, 81a, 84b, 89a–b, 94b; Shebu. 7a, 13a, 35a–b, 38b;
A.Z. 17a, 19b, 64b; Hor. 4a (a rule prohibiting sexual relations with a
menstruating woman does not derive from the Torah), 12a; Zeb. 107a;
Men. 39b, 44a, 45a; Bek. 48a, 49b; Ar. 6b, 7a, 20a; Tem. 3a; Ker. 7a;
Nid. 52a; Meg. 24a (= Sot. 41a); Ber. 19b (= Shab. 81b, 94b;
Er. 41b; Meg. 3b; Men. 37b–38a), Shab. 49b, 56a, 61b (= 116b),
Er. 69a; Pes. 10b, 21b, 22a, 22b (= Qid. 56a; B.Q. 41b; Bek. 6a),
23b, 24a, 24b, 25a, 27a, 29b, 43a–b, 44a–b, 45a, 77b, 78b, 79a, 117a;
Yoma 76a, 85b, 86b, 87a; R.H. 17b; Hag. 12a, 15b; Yeb. 90b, 91a,
94b; Ket. 87b; Ned. 25a, 32a; Naz. 18b, 25b, 37b, 38a; Sot. 2b, 37b;
Git. 2b; Qid. 30a, 35a, 58a, 80b, 81b; B.Q. 87a, 96b, 106a; San. 8b,
21b, 67a, 74a, 90a, 104a; Mak. 16a; Shebu. 12b, 39a; A.Z. 36b, 66a,
69a, 73b; Zeb. 25b (= 109a; Men. 9a, 20a; Bek. 39b; Me. 15b),
102a; Hal. 97b, 98a–b, 99a, 115b, 142a; Bek. 6a; Tem. 3a; Ker. 8b.

The usage, "words" or "matters of Torah," refers to the contents of
revelation, usually in Scripture. "Words of Torah do not receive cultic
contamination" (b. Ber. 22a). People may violate "words" (teachings)
of Torah (Ber. 29b), or be arrested on their account (Ber. 61b). Similar appearances of the usage occur at b. Ber. 61a, 63b; Shab. 12b, 13b
(= Hag. 13a; Men. 45a, in the sense of revealed doctrines), 83b,
88b, 151b; Er. 54a–b, 59a; Suk. 49b; M.Q. 16b; R.H. 19a; Ta. 7a,
28a; Meg. 18b; Hag. 3b, 13a, 14a; Sot. 34a; Qid. 32a; San. 81a; Qid.
40b; B.Q. 61a; San. 90a, 110a (martyrdom for the words of Torah),
Men. 99b; Hul. 136b; Hor. 4b. Israel loves "teachings of Torah" (b.
Men. 18a, 99b).

"Torah" not only "prohibits" or "permits." It also "said" or "says." In
the following we find such usages, all appealing to the Torah as revealed truth, as "said Torah," "and has Torah not said," "for lo, Torah
has said," and the same with "the Torah": Ber. 62b, 63b; Shab. 12a;
Yoma 8a; Men. 36b; Shab. 23a, 25a; Pes. 24a; Shab. 87a, 116a, 119a,
151a; Er. 23b, 56b, 57a, 58a; Yoma 22b, 85b; Suk. 2a, 49b, 52a, 53b;

R.H. 7a; Meg. 29b; Yoma 65b; Ta. 21b; Hag. 17b; Men. 65n; Yeb. 62a, 73b; Ket. 30b, 105a; Ned. 10b, 66b; Naz. 45a; Qid. 57b, 81b; B.Q. 38a, 50b, 112b; San. 19a; B.B. 130b; San. 55a, 72a–b, 73a; Mak. 24a; A.Z. 5b, 51a; Zeb. 41a, 101a, 116a, 120a; Men. 37b, 65b, 103b; Hul. 116b; Bek. 54a; Ar. 16b; Me. 11a; Nid. 31b; Er. 13a; Shab. 13b; Er. 58a; Pes. 43b; Bes. 21a; Ket. 29b; Qid. 64a, 68a; Naz. 38a, 45a; B.Q. 68b; San. 37b; Shebu. 34a; San. 52b, 85b; Mak. 12a; Men. 101a; Hul. 141a; Yoma 67b; Qid. 57b; Hul. 115a, 140a; Bek. 11a; R.H. 16a ("On what account did Torah state" + a verse), Ket. 18a; Git. 51b; B.Q. 107a; B.M. 103a; Shebu. 42b (all: + an established fact of biblical law), Sot. 17a, 46a; Qid. 2b; B.Q. 67b, 68a; San. 112a; Nid. 31b; Mak. 11a; Suk. 53b; Hul. 37a; the Torah has said (+ a verse): Shab. 108a; Yoma 65b; R.H. 7a; Meg. 29b; Naz. 6b, 20a, 25a, 40a; Sot. 16a, 20a; Qid. 50b; B.Q. 83b, 84a; San. 3b, 69a; Zeb. 70a; Men. 81a; Hul. 103a; Ker. 3a; Ber. 58a, 62b; Pes. 27b; Yoma 57a, 85b; Suk. 12a, 37a; Yeb. 25a, 102a; Ket. 17a; Git. 87a; Qid. 73a; B.Q. 34a, 65b, 72b, 84a; San. 9b, 25a, 27a, 63b (Rek. 2b), 65a, 72b; A.Z. 62a; Zeb. 117a; Men. 40b, 98b; Nid. 68b; Git. 89a; "and Torah has said": Shab. 25a, 55a; Shebu. 35b; Tem. 4a; "for Torah has said": Pes. 8b; Sot. 3a; Ar. 16b. These passages do not necessarily cite verses of Scripture verbatim. They may merely allude to explicit facts contained therein. But so far as I can see we never find reference to a teaching otherwise imputed to oral tradition.

Further passages in which "the Torah," or "Torah," is joined to a verb indicating a rule (the Torah "has said," ". . . has applied a strict rule"), and so serves as a source of revelation include these: b. Shab. 70a, 87b, 95b, 96b–97a; b. Pes. 95b; Yoma 44b (the Torah showed concern for Israel's material well-being, so too b. R.H. 27a; Men. 76b, 86b, 88b, 89a; Hul. 49b, 77a), Yoma 51a, 55b, 65b (= 108a), 87b; B.B. 123a, 130a–b; San. 37a, 87b; Shebu. 19b; A.Z. 34a, 52b; Zeb. 53a, 56a; Hul. 24b, 93b; Nid. 11a, 35b; b. Ber. 58a, 62b; Pes. 92b; Ker. 25a; Nid. 17a; Yeb. 63b (the Torah is compared to . . .), Git. 54b; Qid. 24b; B.M. 31a, 89b; Ar. 31a.

It is heresy to deny that the Torah came from heaven (b. San. 99a), but that heresy is readily refuted (b. Men. 60b). One must acknowledge that every detail in the Torah comes from heaven (b. San. 99a). Accordingly, finding "in the Torah" or "in the entire Torah" various facts further indicates that the Torah serves as a source of revealed truth, as at the following: b. Shab. 83b; b. Ket. 46a; Ned. 72b; Naz. 37b; Sot. 3a, Qid. 35a; Mak. 11a; Qid. 39b (keeping all the command- ments in the Torah), 43a; B.Q. 79a; B.M. 71b; B.B. 130b; San. 27a (to be invalid for all purposes of the Torah), Mak. 13b, 24a; Shebu. 14b, 19b, 21b, 26a–b, 29a, 37a; Hor. 3b; Zeb. 17b, 37b (= 57a), 49b, 57a; Men. 91b; Hul. 5a (confessing or rejecting the entire Torah), Nid. 3b, 43a. Those who deny the Torah go to Gehenna (b. Suk. 17a).

Further references to the revelation ("giving") of the Torah occur as follows: b. Ber. 6b, 58a; Pes. 118a; Suk. 13a (= Hal. 62b), A.Z. 9a, 24a; Zeb. 116a; Hul. 101b. The foregoing refer chiefly to the time at which Torah was given, that is, to the age commencing then. "To- rah" was revealed ("given") not to angels (b. Me. 14b) but to mortals (b. Ber. 25b = b. Qid. 54a). God did not withhold Torah from Is- rael (b. Ber. 28a). Furthermore, Torah speaks in language intelligible to humanity (b. Ber. 32b). Moses went up to heaven to receive it (b. Shab. 88b). Israel accepted or received Torah, meaning revelation, so b. Shab. 129b. Moses learned and forgot, so God gave Torah to him as a gift (b. Ned. 38a). "Receiving Torah" as authoritative revelation at Sinai occurs at b. Sot. 12b; b. Shab. 88a; A.Z. 2b. Torah was "given" to Israel, so b. Ber. 63b; b. Er. 21b, 54a; Pes. 68b; Pes. 118a (after 26 generations), b. Ta. 7a, 8a, 25a; to Israel alone as Moses' heirs, so b. Ned. 38a. The giving of the Torah took forty days, b. Sot. 42b; b. Men. 99b. Ezra would have been equally suitable to receive it (b. San. 21b), so too Aqiba (b. Men. 29b). The revelation took place on the Sabbath (b. Shab. 86b). Moses received the Torah in a state of ho- liness (b. Yoma 4a). Israel received it in awe (b. Yoma 4b). When the Torah was given to Israel, the sound traveled through the world (b. Zeb. 116a). It was given only one time (b. Men. 101b), in all lan- guages (b. Sot. 33a).

"Torah" is joined to a possessive referring to God (e.g., God speaks of "my Torah") in the following passages: b. A.Z. 3a; Ber. 11b ("the words of your Torah"), 16b, 17a, 20b, 31b, 60b, 63a (= Tam. 27b); Yoma 87b; R.H. 35a, "this Torah" means God's at b. Ber. 11a. "His Torah" refers to that revealed by God through Moses at b. B.M. 75b; B.B. 74a; San. 110a–b.

A synonym for Torah as revelation is the *Aramaic word* for *instruc- tion*. This occurs in the following passages: b. Ber. 48a; Yoma 87b (to go and study *Oraita* in Babylonia), Ta. 3b, 18a; R.H. 19a; Ned. 50b;

B.M. 84a. "A new [passage of] instruction" in the sense of authoritative teaching is the usage at Sheq. 3:2. "The instruction [Torah] of Moses"—hence, Torah—appears at b. Shab. 116b.

Various passages take for granted that "Torah" means revelation, rather than a particular object. For example, "Torah" was one of seven things created before the creation of the world (b. Pes. 54a; b. Ned. 39b). On account of Torah, heaven and earth endure (b. Pes. 68b; Ned. 32a). Torah serves as a wall around Israel, b. Pes. 87a; b. Bes. 25b; b. B.B. 7b, and as a shield for the world (b. Sot. 21a) and stands up for those who study it (b. Qid. 33b). Torah governs for 2,000 years, between the age of chaos and the age of the Messiah (b. San. 97b; b. A.Z. 9a). Torah is to be interpreted, so that it will reveal its secrets (b. Pes. 119a; Hag. 13a). The whole of the Torah was stated in all languages (b. Ber. 13a). The basic principle of the Torah may be located in a single short passage (b. Ber. 63a). Such fundamentals occur in a given sort of law (b. Shab. 32a; Hag. 11b; Hul. 60b; Ker. 5a).

TORAH AS A PARTICULAR ACT.
AS GENERIC

Sages should "teach Torah" to their children (b. Ber. 8a; b. Suk. 42a) or to others in general (b. Ber. 11b, cf. also b. Ber. 13b, 21b; b. R.H. 23a). "Study of Torah" sets the occasion of a blessing (b. Ber. 21a). "Torah" is as beloved to those who study it as it was on the very day on which it was revealed ("given") (b. Ber. 63b). "Receiving Torah" in the sense of studying it occurs at b. Shab. 86b; b. Qid. 30a. We find allusion to the act of Torah-study at b. B.Q. 17a; Er. 27a, 63b; Qid. 34a–b, 35a, 40a; Meg. 3a–b, 16b; San. 44b; Ket. 17a; b. Ber. 20b, 47b; b. Shab. 127a (the reward of Torah-study lasts for the world to come), b. Pes. 113a; b. Bes. 16a; Ned. 38b. Further references to studying or teaching Torah (*Talmud Torah*) occur at b. Er. 47a; b. Hag. 3b; b. Sot. 22a, 35b, 49b (= b. B.Q. 83a as distinct from studying wisdom), b. Git. 57b; b. Qid. 29 a–b (the father must teach Torah to the son), 30 a–b, 31a, 82b; b. B.M. 85a, 107b; b. R.B. 21a, 144b; b. San. 19b, 68a, 96b, 99a, 101b; b. Shebu. 3b; b. A.Z., 13a; b. Tem. 15b (studying like Moses our rabbi). One studies Torah in a state of purity (b. Men. 110a; b. Yoma 72b). He does so perpetually, that is, reciting Torah-statements as he walks along (b. Yoma

86a; b. Suk. 28a; Ta. 20b, 28a. One should not "go three days without Torah" (b. B.Q. 82b).

In the following passages, "in the Torah" is joined to "study" or "labor" or equivalent verbs, meaning "studying what is found in the Torah": b. Ber. 3b, 5a, 6a, 8a, 10b, 17a, 32b, 61b, 63b, 64a (one who . . . receives the presence of God), Shab. 11a, 30a, 83b, 127b; Er. 21b, 54a–b; Pes. 49b, 50b (= Naz. 23b; Sot. 22b, 47a; San. 35b; Hor. 10b; Ar. 16b), 88a; Yoma 9b, 35b, 72b (those who are occupied with Torah should also fear heaven), Suk. 28a; R.H. 18a (= b. Yeb. 105a); Ta. 7a–b (= b. Meg. 11a), 18a; Meg. 15b, 27a; M.Q. 16b; Hag. 3b, 5b, 12b; Yeb. 63b ("my soul yearns for Torah," meaning, full-time study), Ket. 40a, 77b, 104a, 108b; Sot. 21a, 46b, 49a; Qid. 29b, 30b, 33b; B.Q. 17a, 38a; B.B. 134a, 140b, 141a; San. 20a, 49a, 59a, 70b, 98b, 99a–b; Mak. 10a; A.Z. 2b, 3a–b, 4b, 5b, 17b, 18a, 19a; Men. 110a; Ar. 15b; Tam. 32a.

Further allusions to being occupied with words of Torah, meaning with study, occur at b. Ber. 3b, 11b, 21b, 22a, 24b, 25a; Meg. 6b, 12b; M.Q. 15a; Hag. 14a; Yeb. 105a, 117a; Sot. 13b; Shebu. 15b; Ber. 38b (rising up in the morning for matters of Torah = to study), San. 49a; b. Ber. 14a (one who takes an oath not to study), 63a; Hag. 12b (A.Z. 3b), separating oneself from words of Torah (b. B.B. 79a; San. 106a; Bek. 5b; A.Z. 3b; Shab. 83b).

Studying *oraita*, meaning *Torah*, appears at b. Pes. 88a; Ta. 9b, 21a; Hag. 15a; San. 88b; A.Z. 17b. There is a time for prayer and a time for Torah, meaning Torah-study (b. Shab. 10a). One should set up a regular schedule "for Torah," meaning for study (b. Shab. 31a; Er. 54b). One who fails to use time to study Torah commits an act of nullification of the Torah or of failure to study or cessation from study (*bittul Torah*), at b. Ber. 5a, 22a; Shab. 32b–33a (the transgression of failure to study Torah), Ta. 7b; Hag. 5a; B.M. 84b; A.Z. 18b.

Torah as a corpus of doctrine was neglected before Solomon, Yeb. 21a. So people did not study or keep it.

People memorize Torah through mnemonics, so b. Er. 54b. One learns through perpetual repetition (b. Qid. 30a). They repeat Torah-traditions (b. Qid. 49a). One must preserve his [knowledge of] Torah, which will sustain his life (b. Men. 99b). One should study Torah for its own sake (not to receive a reward), and that is "Torah that expresses faithfulness (*hesed*)" (b. Suk. 49b). One should not benefit from his knowledge of Torah (b. Ned. 55a, 62a). But people pay honor to the Torah (b. Shab. 119a), and that includes sages.

If a person is humble, he will find it easier to learn Torah, receiving it as a gift (b. Ned. 55a; b. Ta. 7a–b). He should work like a simpleton, a dumb ox (b. A.Z. 5b). The best way to preserve "words of Torah" one has learned is through absolute humility (nakedness) on their account (b. Sot. 21b). He must be prepared to stumble (b. Git. 63a) and give his life (b. Git. 57b).

"Torah" is learned through vigorous give-and-take—the war of the Torah (b. Ta. 15b; b. Hag. 14a; b. San. 40b, 93b, 111b). Torah is best learned through service of a master. One "gives" in Torah-study (b. Ber. 56b). When they "learn Torah," disciples should remain standing (b. Ta. 21a).

Torah may not only be learned but also forgotten (b. Shab. 138b; Er. 54a; b. Ket. 103b; b. B.M. 21a; b. San. 99a; b. Hag. 15a). Therefore one should keep learning from youth to old age (b. Yeb. 62b) and do so regularly (b. San. 99b). One will continually engage in reflection on Torah (b. Ber. 24b). Disciples should discuss matters of Torah as they walk along (b. Ta. 10b; Sot. 49a). One ceases to study Torah only at death (b. Shab. 30a).

"Learning" is distinct from reflection on what is learned, so b. Ber. 63b. One learns Torah best in connection with a passage which interests him (b. A.Z. 19a). Beyond reflection, there is expert exegesis of Torah, as at b. Qid. 10b, meaning the capacity to penetrate the Torah's secrets (b. Pes. 119a; b. San. 21b, 102a).

References to going or coming to study Torah with a particular sage occur as follows: b. Ber. 34b, 63a; b. Shab. 147b; b. Er. 11b, 47b, 53a, 54b, 91a; b. Yoma 35a, b, 79b; b. Ta. 29a; b. Hag. 15a; b. Yeb. 15b, 84a, 105b; b. Naz. 49b; b. Sot. 10b (studying Torah with a social inferior), 20a; b. Qid. 52b; b. B.Q. 70a; b. B.M. 58b; b. B.B. 8a (sages cutting their feet on journeys from town to town to study Torah), 56b; b. San. 68a; b. Shebu. 13a; b. Men. 72a; b. Tem. 16a (the eyes of both master and disciple are illumined when the disciple goes to the master). One goes into exile to a "place of Torah" (b. Pes. 49a). One "acquires the Torah," meaning mastering traditions in the company of others (b. Ber. 63b).

Great scholars enhance the Torah as they study it (b. Shab. 145b). They teach Torah in public (b. Ta. 6a; b. San. 5a; b. Hor. 11b). There are references to study-houses (b. Bes. 44a). One appropriate verb is "to spread" or "scatter Torah": b. Ta. 29a; b. M.Q. 25a; b. B.M. 85b; b. Tem. 16a. Torah also "goes forth," e.g., from the sons of the poor, meaning that they become disciples and masters (b. Ned. 81a). The great sage may resemble a ministering angel (b. M.Q. 17a; Hag. 15b), in which case disciples will seek him out and study Torah as he states it. It is best to study with one master (b. A.Z. 19a) and learn his traditions. What sages teach is called "torah," as much as what God revealed (b. Yoma 28b: "the torah of his master").

Relationships between disciple and master are modeled on those between child and parent (b. M.Q. 26a). Insufficient discipleship leads to imperfect learning and, hence, schism (b. Sot. 47 a; b. San. 88b). If one teaches Torah to another, he enters the status of the father of the disciple (b. San. 19b, 99b). But masters also learn "Torah" from disciples (b. Mak. 10a). One may be a disciple in that he "learns Torah" and a master in that he makes decisions—both in relationship to the same other man (b. R.H. 25b). Slaves are not to be taught Torah (b. Ket. 28a). They cannot become disciples.

What one has learned or has taught is called "his Torah" at b. Ber. 57a; Shab. 10a (doing one's Torah, meaning studying), Er. 54b; A.Z. 19a; Ta. 7a; M.Q. 16b; Hag. 15a; San. 71a, 102a, 106b; Men. 29b, 99b; Qid. 81a; San. 99b; Shab. 33b; San. 38b; A.Z. 5a (to rejoice at the Torah [= learning and teaching] of a rabbi), Pes. 112b; Hag. 15b (remember his *torah*, not his deeds), Yoma 28b; Yeb. 96b. References to "their Torah" meaning "their act of study" or "what they have learned" occur at b. Ber. 32b, 35b; Er. 53a; Shab. 11a ("their act of study" is their occupation). Torah-study protects the building in which it takes place (b. Er. 18b). One may achieve atonement "in Torah" (b. Suk. 18a; Yeb. 105a), meaning in Torah-study. "Torah" is comparable to a healing medicine (b. Qid. 30b). Inadequate study led to schism, called "two Torahs" (b. Sot. 47b; San. 88b). Israel's enemies make decrees against the study of Torah (b. B.B. 60b; b. Ber. 61b; Ta. 18a). But gentiles also tell Israelites, "Teach us your Torah" (b. B.Q. 38a). They may refer to "your Torah" in the sense of "your revealed doctrine," as at b. Ber. 32b; R.H. 17b; A.Z. 17a, 54b, 55a. Many of these usages already have been illustrated in the exegetical collection cited in earlier chapters.

As Generic: "Torah" in the sense of categorical rule or classification appears at the following passages: b. Zeb. 69b (Hul. 27b), Ket. 105a;

B.B. 72b; Ned. 25a; Shebu. 29a; Men. 110a; Zeb. 48a; Ker. 22b; Suk. 31b; A.Z. 16a; San. 112b; Tem. 8a; Git. 8a; Er. 70b; Pes. 98b; B.B. 72b; Sot. 43b; Qid. 41b, 59b; Git. 23b, 78b; M.Q. 13b; Men. 21a; B.M. 62b; Er. 19b, 59b, 60a; Shebu. 29a; Men. 3b, 4a, 11–a; Pes. 51a; Bekh. 27a; Men. 18b; Yeb. 86b, 97b; Ket. 26a; Naz. 16b (falling into the torah = category of uncleanness, not "the torah" of an offering), Ber. 23b; B.M. 51a, 52b, 57a–b (= Tem. 27b), Men. 82a; Shab. 28b (the status of utensil), 46a–b, 81b, 124a, 126b; Er. 12a; Bes. 10a, 23b; B.Q. 67a; B.B. 66b; A.Z. 16a; Qid. 8a; Er. 5a, 25a; Suk. 14a; B.B. 107b; Ned. 25a; Men. 3b, 19a–b; B.M. 4a; Naz. 6b, 20a; Bek. 18b; Suk. 19a; B.M. 112a; Mak. 2a; B.B. 72b; Er. 19b, 64a, 70a, 71b, 73b, 79b; Qid. 13a; B.M. 62a; Ned. 44a; Er. 59b (category of a door), Men. 18b; Qid. 13a, 50b, 59a, 76a; Ber. 23b (an argument in the category of *a fortiori* arguments), Yeb. 86b; Naz. 16b; Qid. 23b; Zeb. 38a; B.Q. 93a; Er. 57a; B.B. 72b; B.M. 65a; Tem. 6b; San. 109a; Git. 23b; A.Z. 72a; Ket. 105a; Qid. 59b (status of agent), B.Q. 93a; Ar. 19a; Er. 6a–b, 8a–b, 15b (the law governing the gossip).

TORAH AS INDICATOR OF STATUS

Both human beings and also teachings enter into the status of "Torah" or are denied that status. Particular rules or opinions may be attributed to "Torah" or to "scribes" (in Aramaic: rabbis) and so distinguished as to their status. This use of the word Torah and its Aramaic equivalent, *oraita*, is extremely frequent in the Talmud of Babylonia. Let us consider how that Talmud sorts out the status or authority of diverse opinions or rules and then turn to how it imputes to human beings the status of torah.

The distinction between a rule deriving from the authority of Torah, meaning Scripture, and one based on the authority of scribes occurs at b. Er. 31b, 35b, 58b, 77a, 85b; b. Suk. 5a, 13a; b. Yeb. 36b; Ket. 56a, 83b, 84a; Zeb. 101a; b. B.M. 55b, 61b; b. Shebu. 7a; b. Zeb. 101a (= b. R.H. 19a; Ta. 17b; Yeb. 85b: scribes' rulings demand more stringent enforcement than Torah's rulings). There are details of rules deriving from the Torah as distinct from details of rules deriving from scribes (b. Suk. 28a; b. B.B. 134a; b. Meg. 19b). Along these same lines, a teaching may derive not from the Torah of Moses but from the words of Ezekiel (b. San. 22b, 83b; Yoma 71b; M.Q. 5a; Zeb. 18b, 22b) or from received tradition (b. R.H. 7a; Ta.

17b). An explicit distinction is contained in the statement, "Were their statement not a matter of Torah, while the statement of my master is a matter of tradition . . ." (b. Hul. 137a). "Words of Torah" within an otherwise secular word are recognized at b. Shab. 30b for Qohelet. Sages may enforce their rulings *over* those of Torah (b. Er. 81b). The language of sages is differentiated from the language of the Torah (b. A.Z. 58b; Hul. 137b; b. Pes. 87b).

The expression, "as a matter of Torah" carries the sense "the rule so far as the Torah lays it down," in contradistinction to the position of some other layer of authority. We find this usage at b. Ber. 19b, 20b (Shebu. 20b), Shab. 48b, 58b, 145a, 146a; Er. 4b, 17b, 81b; Suk. 6b; Yeb. 78a; Nid. 67b; Pes. 43b, 91b, 92a; Yeb. 7b; Zeb. 32b; Yeb. 72a, 102a, 105b, 113b, 122b; Ket. 57b, 102a; Ned. 45a; Naz. 45a; Naz. 41a; Git. 4a, 50a, 53a, 55a, 88b; Qid. 17b, 18a, 39a, 73a; B.Q. 94b; B.M. 57a; Tem. 27a; B.B. 48a, 114b, 175b; Hul. 122a; Bekh. 51a; Tem. 27a; Me. 2a–b, 12a, 15a; Nid. 25a. These entries rarely include a citation of a biblical verse.

Proving a given proposition "from the Torah" means demonstrating that the rule enjoys the authority of revelation, and not the lesser standing of a decree of scribes. References to demonstrating "from the Torah" that such-and-so is the case include the following: b. Ber. 10a, 15b (= b. Pes. 68a), 21a–b, 48b, 52b, 62b, 69a; b. Shab. 103b; Ta. 2b, 105a, 114a; Er. 36a; Pes. 18b, 66b; Yoma 39a, 51a, 73b, 74a; Suk. 41a, 43a–b, 44a; R.H. 32a; Bes. 15b; M.Q. 5a, 18b; Hag. 24a; Sot. 29b; Yeb. 4a, 12b, 21a, 34b, 54a–b, 89b (removing a principle from the Torah), 90b, 92b; Ket. 10a, 22a, 111b; Ned. 39b; Naz. 29a; Sot. 7a, 20b, 29a, 65a, 83a, 90b; Qid. 27b, 28b, 64a, 71a, 80b (= San. 21b; A.Z. 36b); B.M. 32a (a commandment deriving from the Torah), 46b, 47b, 57b, 93a; B.B. 69b, 147a; San. 10a (= Mak. 2b), 17b, 40b, 46b, 90a (to uproot a matter from the Torah), 90b, 91a–b, 92a, 101a, 104b; Mak. 2b, 10b; Shebu. 18b; A.Z. 27a–b; Men. 32a, 68b; Hul. 4a (= 27b), 17b, 20a–b, 27b, 28a, 42a, 64b, 85b, 86a, 92b, 98a, 104a, 106a, 116a, 139b; Bek. 13b, 50a; Ar. 11a, 6b; Tem. 29a, 32b; Nid. 30b. The view that a rule is a law revealed to Moses at Sinai (b. Nid. 45a) implies the same distinction. This distinction forms one of the basic heuristic methods of the Talmud of Babylonia, which, time and again, wants to know whether a given rule enjoys the status of Torah-law or scribal-law, Torah- or rabbinical-authority. Many sustained discussions begin with precisely that question. Yet it is difficult to see how the question has not originated, if in much simpler form, in the Mishnah's distinction.

Further points at which a teaching of Torah is distinguished from a teaching of scribes or sages or "of them" are at the following: b. Ta. 17b, 28a; Yeb. 85b; Hag. 10b; Yeb. 90b; San. 46a; B.M. 88a; Hul. 137a; Nid. 23a, 50a; R.H. 19a; B.Q. 82b; Shab. 58a (= Men. 69b), 96a; Er. 21a; R.H. 34a; Yeb. 40b, 41a, 44a; Ket. 10a; Naz. 58b, 59a; Qid. 17b, 77a; San. 87a, 88b; Zeb. 99b, 100b; Hul. 28b, 72b, 104a; Nid. 23a, 69a.

The distinction between a ruling on the authority of rabbis and one based on the authority of the Torah is expressed in Aramaic, *oraita* vs. *rabbanan*, sometimes followed by citation of a biblical verse, at the following passages (among many): Ber. 14a, 15a, 17b, 19b, 20b, 21a, 45b, 46a, 49a; Shab. 14b, 16a–b, 18a, 24a, 46b, 27b, 128b, 148b; Er. 2a (= Suk. 2a), 3a, 4a–b, 11b, 12b, 32a, 35b, 36a, 47a, 78a, 79b, 85b, 87a, and so on. Kasovsky (*Concordance*, I. 302–308) lists approximately 450 passages in which the word is used in this way. Furthermore, parallel passages, "in respect to *oraita*," "in *oraita*," "on the authority of . . ." or "in the status of . . ." *oraita*, account for approximately 200 more entries. While we find some usages parallel to "Torah" in the sense of a Torah-scroll or revelation, the bulk of the passages—nearly a third as many occurrences as "Torah"—invoke the principal exegetical distinction between Torah-authority and (in Hebrew) scribes', or (in Aramaic) rabbis', authority.

"Torah" serves as a source of specified measurements at b. Pes. 109a; b. B.B. 58b; b. San. 76b; b. Ker. 27a; Qid. 11a–b, B.Q. 36b; Bek. 50a–b; Shebu. 20a. But these references commonly mean that a given measurement has the status of Torah-authority and not the lesser status of scribes' or rabbis' authority. A transaction valid beyond cavil will have the standing of a transaction in accord with Torah, as at b. Git. 89b, an act of consecration in accordance with the Torah. One should "make a fence" for the Torah (b. Yeb. 90b; San. 46a). But "A ruling in accordance with Torah law in particular" (*din Torah*) is too strict and unwise (b. B.M. 30b; b. San. 6a). Rulings of a more moderate nature are advisable.

Repeating "Torah" is distinguished from "laws," though how the two relate is unclear to me (b. Qid. 49a). When Torah-status applies to a man, it means that that man has attained not only learning but learning gained in the right way. The result is a shift in the man's status, not merely an increase in what he knows. To be sure, Torah in the sense of learning, quite separate from status, is always present in these same usages. But at issue are references to Torah in which the matter of learning is secondary, the issue of one's standing or supernatural condition, primary. A person may bless another with Torah as distinct from wealth, children, and long life (b. Ta. 6a). It seems to me that what is asked is mastery of traditions and enjoyment of high standing on that account. Torah in the sense of achievement in learning and associated merit occurs in such phrases as, "Such is Torah and such is the reward [for learning]?" (b. Ber. 61b). Also "handsome Torah in an ugly container" (b. Ned. 50b) bears this same enlarged meaning. Torah is contrasted with worldly standing or greatness (b. Git. 59a); the two rarely coincide (b. San. 36a). Blessing someone "with Torah" (b. Ta. 6a; Tem. 16a) means to wish that person achievement in learning. "A man great in Torah" occurs at b. Ta. 10b. Abraham, Isaac and Jacob were "powerful" in Torah (b. Sot. 14a). Doeg was great in Torah (b. San. 106b). Torah in the sense of merit acquired through learning further occurs at b. Ber. 6b, 57a; Shab. 63a.

Those who study Torah are called "sons of Torah": Shab. 139a–b, 145b; Yeb. 46a; A.Z. 58a, 59a; Er. 40a. This constitutes a distinctive status at b. Yeb. 46a; A.Z. 59a. A town may or may not enjoy the same status, A.Z. 58a, 59a, depending on the character of the residents. Knowledge of Torah is what distinguishes a person (b. Qid. 33a). One who teaches Torah in this world will do so in the next (b. San. 92a). One who sacrifices to study Torah in this world will learn mysteries from God in the world to come (b. Hag. 14a). The honor due to, or deriving from, Torah (= learning) occurs at the following passages: b. Meg. 3b, 23a; b. Ber. 63b; b. B.B. 8a (not deriving benefit from the honor accruing to the Torah). If a man wishes to ensure that Torah not cease among his offspring, he should marry the daughter of a disciple of a sage (Yoma 71a). If one is devoted to study of Torah in this world and sacrifices on that account, he will become great in the world to come (b. B.M. 85b). A similar promise occurs at b. San. 100a.

Sages erred if they boasted or took pride in themselves for having mastered Torah (b. Ta. 20a). They also must not make private use of "the light of Torah" (b. Ket. 111b). Sages further erred if they supposed that having "learned Torah" they were free of punishment for sinning in some other way (b. Sot. 4b; b. San. 99a). But a transgression will not wipe out the value of "Torah" (b. Sot. 21a). One must make himself small "in Torah" (b. Meg. 11a), that is, be modest so as to learn.

WRITTEN AND ORAL TORAH

"Torah" refers specifically to Scripture as written Torah at b. Ber. 5a; b. Qid. 30a. The greater part of the Torah was given in writing, the lesser part orally (b. Git. 60b). The distinction between written and oral Torah, with stress on revelation of two Torahs at Sinai, appears at the following passages: b. Shab. 31a; b. Yoma 28b; b. Qid. 66a. All three references occur in stories about conflicts or heresy. This myth certainly is distinctive to the sages' circles. The "complete Torah" that is "ours," b. Men. 65b; b. B.B. 116a, contains a possible allusion to the myth of the dual Torah, also in the setting of controversy, now between Pharisees and Sadducees. Apart from these we find no reference to the conception of a written and an oral Torah revealed at Sinai. We find no passage in which the Mishnah as such is described as oral Torah, or in which the teachings of scribes or rabbis are called "oral Torah." Such teachings are called torah, that is, part of revelation, in the generic sense alone.

The claim that in the first century B.C.E. (and long before) Jews believed in the myth of the two Torahs is generally accompanied by citation of the following story.

B. Shabbat 31a
[Translated by H. Freedman, pp. 139–40]

Our Rabbis taught: A certain heathen once came before Shammai and asked him, 'How many Torahs have you?'

'Two,' he replied: 'the Written Torah and the Oral Torah.'

'I believe you with respect to the Written, but not with respect to the Oral Torah; make me a proselyte on condition that you teach me the Written Torah [only].' [But] he scolded and repulsed him in anger.

When he went before Hillel, he accepted him as a proselyte. On the first day he taught him, Alef, beth, gimmel, daleth; the following day he reversed [them] to him.

'But yesterday you did not teach them to me thus,' he protested.

'Must you then not rely upon me? Then rely upon me with respect to the Oral [Torah] too.'

The foregoing passage is most commonly cited as evidence of belief from very early times in the doctrine of the two Torahs. Since it speaks of Hillel, it is conventionally assumed that people in the time of Hillel held such beliefs. But, as we have observed, the story occurs for the first time only in the final composition of the entire rabbinic canon. Standing by itself, it demonstrates only that at ca. 500 C.E., people not only believed in the myth of the two Torahs but ascribed that conviction also to Hillel. The lack of evidence in the Mishnaic sector of the canon that people knew about the myth of the two Torahs hardly enhances the credibility of the tale as an account of something that really happened in Hillel's day. Nor does it testify to convictions held during five hundred years thereafter.

THE TORAH AS A WAY OF LIFE

"Torah" was one of three gifts God gave to Israel, b. Ber. 5a, the others being the land of Israel and the world to come. Here, Torah hardly demands so narrow an interpretation as "revelation." "Truth" refers to "Torah" in the same context. A more striking usage is implicit in the words "service of," or "to," "Torah," b. Ber. 7b, meaning a life of discipleship to a great master, or exemplar, or Torah. So a master may be identified with "Torah" in his person (b. Hor. 13b). The Torah as a way of life is compared to a yoke, which guides a creature (b. San. 94b). Carrying out the entire Torah from A to Z (b. Shab. 55a) surely involves this same notion of Torah as a way of life. Abraham did so (b. Yoma 28b). A disciple of a sage may depart from the Torah (b. Hag. 9b). One may carry out "the entire Torah" (b. Qid. 39b). By rejecting idolatry, one confesses to the truth of the entire Torah (b. Qid. 40a). These references cannot apply only to the contents but must encompass the way of life of Torah. "Restoring the Torah to its proper status" (b. Qid. 66a) involved a reform of the national life. Carrying out "the entire Torah" (b. A.Z. 3a, 4a) and accepting it all (b. A.Z. 5a) bear the same broad meaning.

"Torah" in the broad sense of guidance for life, in situations not explicitly described in Scripture, occurs at b. Ber. 62a; Meg. 28a; Er.

100b (Torah teaches modest conduct), Yoma 4b, 75b; b. Bes. 25b. One who studies Torah does things in a desirable way (b. Yoma 86a), and Torah serves as the antidote to illicit desires (b. Ber. 16a). "Torah" leads to scrupulousness (b. A.Z. 20b).

Living in accord with the Torah and doing commandments protects people (b. Ber. 31a; b. Bes. 25b). One should strengthen commitment to Torah, good deeds, prayer, and proper conduct (b. Ber. 32b). Here "Torah" may stand for the component of Torah-study in the holy way of life. "Torah and good deeds" joined together surely means Torah as learning in particular (b. Ber. 61a). So too "Torah" is contrasted to "fear of Heaven" (b. Shab. 31a). Here too, learning is not enough, so "Torah" stands for learning, not for the whole holy way of life. The same is so when Torah contrasts with right action (b. Shab. 114a). But the letters of the word Torah add up to 611, that is, nearly the (mythic) number of commandments (b. Mak. 23b), so the commandments and Torah look to be one and the same—the whole a holy way of life. "Torah" teaches proper conduct (b. Men. 84a). For example, one should engage in Torah rather than drink wine (b. Shab. 10a).

There can be infidels, specifically those who deny "the Torah" (b. Suk. 17a). Denying the Torah is tantamount to idolatry (b. Ned. 25a). For its part, Israel has the possibility of "forgetting Torah" (b. Suk. 20a; B.M. 85b; Sot. 48a; b. San. 97a; b. Tem. 14b). "If such-and-such happens, what will become of Torah?" (b. Ber. 35b; b. Shab. 88b) bears this same ambiguous meaning: the contents of revelation, but also the way of life decreed therein. When the great masters do not cooperate or perish, again "what will become of Torah?" (b. Naz. 50a), here too meaning that the learning, but with it also the way of life, will be endangered. "The Torah" may be more beloved to one generation than to another (b. Ber. 63a). Likewise one may be suspected of not observing a detail of the Torah (b. Er. 69a), in which case he is suspect in regard to the entire Torah—surely this means the way of life (cf. b. Hal. 4b–5a). One may also deny "the Torah of Moses your rabbi" (b. San. 106a), which means to apostatize.

TORAH AS A SOURCE OF SALVATION

Our rapid survey of the Babylonian Talmud's uses of the word Torah, as indicated by concordance data, points to a far richer and more varied corpus of examples than we have seen in earlier compilations. But these examples fall into established classification, at best speciating a known genus in predictable ways. The Babylonian Talmud, however, extends the limits of already familiar ground— instances where the word Torah connotes the salvation of both the individual and the nation of Israel. The former sense of the word— personal reward for study of Torah, in this world and the next— surely strikes us as familiar. Abot's emphasis upon the direct encounter with God involved in study of Torah reflects one principal assertion. When a man studies Torah, his status on earth and in heaven undergoes an important change. The latter sense, the notion that the people Israel will be saved through study of Torah, or that "words of Torah" settle the fate of Israel, first appears, so it would seem, in the Talmud of the Land of Israel. From that point onward, however, this, too, defines a commonplace taxon of the word Torah.

While both the national and the individual dimensions of salvation mark the measure of the word Torah in the Babylonian Talmud, the national proves the more interesting. For the notion of private salvation through "Torah" study and practice, of which we hear much, presents no surprise. When, by contrast, we find God saying, "If a man occupies himself with the study of Torah, works of charity, and prays with the community, I account it to him as if he had redeemed me and my children from among the nations of the world" (b. Ber. 8a), we confront a concept beyond the imagination of the framers of Abot and the other compositions of that circle. Still more indicative of the importance for Israel as a whole, imputed to Torah-learning, is the view that those who master the Torah do not require protection by this-worldly means. Rabbis need not contribute to the upkeep of the walls of a town, "because rabbis do not require protection" (b. B.B. 8a). Sayings such as these focus to be sure upon the individual who has mastered the Torah. But the supernatural power associated with the Torah here is thought to protect not the individual alone, but Israelites in general associated with the individual Torah-master. So, given the social perspective of our sages, all Israel enjoys salvation through the Torah.

Of still greater interest, in the Talmud of Babylonia, study of the Torah takes the place of offering sacrifices in the Temple. Indeed, if a person studies the Torah, it is "as if" he has rebuilt the Temple:

B. Sanhedrin 99b
[Translated by H. Freedman, p. 675]

R. Alexandri said: He who studies the Torah for its own sake makes peace in the Upper Family and the Lower Family [men], as it is written, *Or let him take hold of my strength* [i.e., the Torah], *that he may make peace with me; and he shall make peace with me* (Is. 27:5). Rab said: It is as though he built the heavenly and the earthly Temples, as it is written, *And I have put my words in thy mouth, and I have covered thee in the shadow of mine hand, that I may plant the heavens, and lay the foundations of the earth, and say unto Zion, Thou art my people* (Is. 51:16). R. Johanan said: He also shields the whole world [from the consequences of its sins], for it is written, *and I have covered* [i.e., protected] *thee in the shadow of mine hand.* Levi said: He also hastens the redemption, as it is written, *and say unto Zion, Thou art my people.*

B. Sanhedrin 44b
[Translated by Jacob Schachter, p. 290]

R. Samuel b. Unia said in the name of Rab: The study of the Torah is more important than the offering of the daily whole offering.

The assertions in these pericopae take on more concrete meaning in light of yet another story. The house of Eli's iniquity "will not be expiated with sacrifice or offering for ever" (1 Sam. 3:14), on which Rabbah said, "Not with sacrifice or offering but with words of the Torah" (b. Yeb. 105a). True, study of Torah by itself would never suffice; acts of lovingkindness also must accompany learning. But the striking comparison between sacrifice and study of Torah makes the main point. The study of Torah substitutes for the ancient cult and does for Israel now what sacrifice did then: reconcile Israel to its Father in heaven, wipe away sin, secure atonement, so save Israel. These deeply mythic convictions give concrete expression to the view that the Torah not only sanctifies, but also saves, Israel. In the later history of Judaism, they became clichés. But once they were new and amazing claims, and this happened, as we have seen, in the second stage of the formation of Judaism.

The dimensions of Torah-learning therefore no longer were bounded by the limits of the individual and his fate. Now they encompassed the life of Israel, the nation, and so spoke of the ongoing concern for the destroyed Temple and its cult. When, further, we consider that Temple and cult now formed central images in the expression of the messianic hope, with one important task of the Messiah conceived as the rebuilding of the Temple and the renewal of the sacrifices, the picture becomes fully clear. Through studying the Torah, the disciple took his place in the messianic process. His action bore the promise of rebuilding the Temple, that is to say, bringing the Messiah. His act of learning was to be compared to an act of sacrifice in the cult, that is to say, a foretaste of the messianic time to come. Accordingly, it required no great step from assertions such as these to the further conclusion that, as a symbol, the Torah bore within itself the entire teleological system of Judaism. Torah-study stood not only for things to be learned or done in the here and now. It pointed also—even here and now—toward the coming of the Messiah. So when we speak of the Torah as a source of salvation, we address very concrete and specific claims, hence expectations, and not merely generalized convictions about the worth of the rabbinic system as a whole.

Torah affords protection not only in time to come, but even now, a view expressed both in abstract terms, as we have seen, and also in concrete ones. Studying the teachings of the Torah deflects those who do so from paths leading to death to paths of life (b. Hag. 3b) and protects the disciple both in youth and in old age (b. Qid. 82b). These rather philosophical statements, however, do not reveal the practicality of the protection under discussion here. The following statements prove much more concrete:

B. Erubin 54a
[Translated by Israel W. Slotki, pp. 375–76]

R. Joshua b. Levi stated: If a man is on a journey and has no company let him occupy himself with the study of the Torah, since it is said in Scripture, *For they shall be a chaplet of grace* (Prov. 1:9).

If he feels pains in his head, let him engage in the study of the Torah, since it is said, *For they shall be a chaplet of grace unto thy head.*

If he feels pains in his throat let him engage in the study of the Torah, since it is said, *And chains about thy neck.*

If he feels pains in his bowels, let him engage in the study of the Torah, since it is said, *It shall be a healing to thy navel* (Prov. 3:8).

If he feels pain in his bones, let him engage in the study of the Torah, since it is said, *And marrow to thy bones* (Prov. 3:8).

If he feels pain in all his body, let him engage in the study of the Torah, since it is said, *And healing to all his flesh* (Prov. 4:22).

R. Judah son of R. Hiyya remarked: Come and see how the dispensation of mortals is not like that of the Holy One, blessed be He. In the dispensation of mortals, when a man administers a drug to a fellow it may be beneficial to one limb but injurious to another, but with the Holy One, blessed be He, it is not so. He gave a Torah to Israel and it is a drug of life for all his body, as it is said, *And healing to all his flesh* (Prov. 4:22).

B. Sotah 21a
[Translated by A. Cohen, p. 106]

The following did R. Menahem son of R. Jose expound: *For the commandment is a lamp and Torah is light* (Prov. 6:23)—the verse identifies the commandment with a lamp and Torah with light; the commandment with a lamp to tell thee that as a lamp only protects temporarily, so [the fulfillment of] a commandment only protects temporarily; and Torah with light to tell thee that as light protects permanently, so Torah protects permanently; and it states, *When thou walkest it shall lead thee* (Prov. 6:22)—'when thou walkest it shall lead thee,' viz., in this world; 'when thou sleepest it shall watch over thee,' viz., in death; *and when thou awakest it shall talk with thee,* viz., in the Hereafter.

There is a parable of a man who is walking in the middle of the night and darkness, and is afraid of thorns, pits, thistles, wild beasts and robbers, and also does not know the road in which he is going. If a lighted torch is prepared for him, he is saved from thorns, pits and thistles; but he is still afraid of wild beasts and robbers, and does not know the road in which he is going. When, however, dawn breaks, he is saved from wild beasts and robbers, but still does not know the road in which he is going. When, however, he reaches the cross-roads, he is saved from everything.

The sayings just reviewed assign to the Torah a supernatural or magical power and treat its words as tantamount to prayers or incantations. The main point is that the kind of protection afforded by the Torah proves concrete and specific, immediate and practical. Study of Torah, after all, is as practical as offering an animal for sacrifice—and bears equivalent consequences (b. Ber. 5a).

At the same time the Torah finds a place in the framework of psychological well-being. Specifically, the Torah serves as the antidote for sin: "If you occupy yourselves with the Torah, you will not be delivered into the hand of the desire to do evil" (b. Qid. 30b). The Torah serves, specifically, to control the impulse of human beings to do what they should not. Indeed, the Torah was so shaped as to correspond in its teachings to, and to forestall, the impulses of humanity:

B. Shabbat 88b–89a
[Translated by H. Freedman, pp. 421–23]

R. Joshua b. Levi also said: When Moses ascended on high, the ministering angels spake before the Holy One, blessed be He, 'Sovereign of the Universe! What business has one born of woman amongst us?' 'He has come to receive the Torah,' answered He to them. Said they to Him, 'That secret treasure, which has been hidden by Thee for nine hundred and seventy-four generations before the world was created, Thou desirest to give to flesh and blood! *What is man, that thou art mindful of him, And the son of man, that thou visitest him? O Lord our God, How excellent is thy name in all the earth! Who hast set thy glory* [the Torah] *upon the Heavens!'* (Ps. 8:5,2). 'Return them an answer,' bade the Holy One, blessed be He, to Moses.

'Sovereign of the Universe,' replied he, 'I fear lest they consume me with the [fiery] breath of their mouths.'

'Hold on to the Throne of Glory,' said He to him, 'and return them an answer,' as it is said, *He maketh him to hold on to the face of his throne, And spreadeth his cloud over him* (Job 26:9).

He [then] spake before Him: Sovereign of the Universe! The Torah which Thou givest me, what is written therein? *I am the Lord thy God, which brought thee out of the Land of Egypt* (Ex. 20:2).

Said he to them [the angels], 'Did ye go down to Egypt; were ye enslaved to Pharaoh: why then should the Torah be yours?'

Again, What is written therein? *Thou shalt have none other gods* (Ex. 20:3): do ye dwell among peoples that engage in idol worship?

Again what is written therein? *Remember the Sabbath day, to keep it holy* (Ex. 20:8): do ye then perform work, that ye need to rest?

Again what is written therein? *Thou shalt not take* [tissa] [*the name . . . in vain*] (Ex. 20:7): are there any business dealings among you?

Again what is written therein, *Honour thy father and thy mother* (Ex. 20:12); have ye fathers and mothers?

Again what is written therein? *Thou shalt not murder. Thou shalt not commit adultery. Thou shalt not steal*; is there jealousy among you; is the Evil Tempter among you? Straightway they conceded [right] to the Holy One, blessed be He.

Immediately each one was moved to love [Moses] and transmitted something to him, for it is said, *Thou hast ascended on high, thou hast taken spoils* [the Torah]; *Thou hast received gifts on account of man* (Ps. 68:19): as a recompense for their calling thee man thou didst receive gifts.

The concrete salvation—this-worldly benefit, otherworldly reward—promised by the study of Torah set forth promises to be kept even now, and certainly in time to come. The shape of the program of rewards corresponds to the layout of sacrifices people made for Torah-study. If a disciple studied Torah in poverty, his prayer would be heard (b. Sot. 49a). If he studied when hungry, so that his face became emaciated, in the world to come his face would shine. If he starved himself here, in the next world he would be satisfied (b. San. 100a). A person who meditated on the Torah only in appropriate places—not in filthy alleys—and who did so constantly could be expected to live a long time (b. Meg. 28a). When, therefore, the expectation that Torah-study would endow the disciple with supernatural power was disappointed, people wondered why:

B. Sanhedrin 106b
[Translated by H. Freedman, pp. 727–28]

Raba observed: Is there any greatness in propounding problems? In the years of Rab Judah the whole study was confined to Nezikin, whilst we study a great deal even of 'Ukzin, and when Rab Judah came to the law, 'If a woman preserves vegetables in a pot'—or as others say, 'olives which were preserved with their leaves are clean,'—he observed, 'I see here the discussion of Rab and Samuel'; whilst we, on the other hand, have studied 'Ukzin at thirteen sessions. Yet Rab Judah merely took off his shoes, and the rain came down, whilst we cry out [in supplication] but there is none to heed us. But it is because the Holy One, blessed be He, requires the heart, as it is written, *But the Lord looketh on the heart* (1 Sam. 16:7).

The significance of this complaint that the latter generations know more Torah yet enjoy no supernatural power on that account is self-evident. People took for granted a correlation between mastery of Torah and supernatural power. Accordingly, Torah provided salvific power, both for the people Israel and for the life of the individual and community.

Some solace for the disjuncture between mastery of Torah and the rewards of this life lay in the expectation of what awaited in heaven. Specifically, heaven presented a mirror of earth, the great below being small above. But those who were masters of Torah now would be great there too:

B . Pesahim 50a
[Translated by H. Freedman, p. 239]

R. Joseph the son of R. Joshua b. Levi, became ill and fell into a trance. When he recovered, his father asked him, 'What did you see?'

'I saw a topsy-turvy world,' he replied, 'the upper [class] underneath and the lower on top.'

He replied: 'My son,' he observed, 'you saw a clear world. And how are we [situated] there?'

'Just as we are here, so are we there. And I heard them saying, "Happy is he who comes hither with his learning in his hand."'

Accordingly, the master of Torah, esteemed in this world, would be received in the world to come, even though others who are great in this world would come to nothing after death.

The stories and sayings cited at some length in this chapter, as well as in that surveying the Talmud of the Land of Israel, in some ways stand on a single continuum with the assertions of Abot. But they make claims that the framers of Abot never made. They express expectations for which in Abot we look in vain, even for the individual, of whom Abot does speak. In the two Talmuds the word Torah thus bears not only the entire range of established meanings, but an unanticipated and utterly fresh sense as well. This is in two ways.

First, Abot exhibits no counterpart to the concrete rewards for individual Torah-study laid out in the two Talmuds. What Abot promises is a rather general thing: encounter with the Presence of God. What the Talmuds propose to deliver contrasts in the specificity and concreteness of its character: power to make rain, healing of ailments, deliverance from material woes and for worldly, as well as otherworldly, life.

Second, as I have emphasized, the national and communal character of the salvation afforded in the two Talmuds' conception of the Torah seems to me to lack all precedent in the documents grouped around the Mishnah. The sage, for his part, serves not only himself, as in Abot, but the nation as a whole. The power enjoyed by the sage because of his knowledge of the Torah imparts benefit to the entire nation. It serves much as the cult and sacrifice once did. That, by definition, is service to the nation as a whole. I find no such stress in Abot upon the national dimension of the Torah's salvation.

TORAH AND ISRAEL

The consequence of studying the Torah, moreover, bore important implications for the coming of the Messiah. So the doctrine of the study of Torah quite predictably fell into tandem with the teleology of the system as a whole. Yet we must ask how, in a very specific way, the doctrine accounted for the real, historical and social condition of the nation to whom it was addressed. What did the study of Torah have to do with the material national context of Israel? To this last question, and the evidence of the Talmud of Babylonia concerning the answer, we now turn.

Before turning to the Babylonian Talmud, however, I have to specify the *type* of evidence under discussion. It consists of a single systematic and protracted essay upon the subject at hand, that is, an effort to spell out through a variety of completed pericopae a coherent position on the relationship of Israel to the Torah. Why does such a comprehensive construction seem to me by itself to be probative? The reason is that, when the Talmud of Babylonia presents essays on topics or themes independent of the Mishnah, these appear in some important cases to constitute what we might call encyclopedia articles. That is to say, the framers of such essays assemble materials relevant to a given topic and work out a large statement of what they wish to say on that topic, through the selection and organization of pertinent sayings and stories. Quite separate from the Talmud's systematic constructions that elucidate and amplify a passage of the Mishnah and the legal principles contained therein, these autonomous essays prove more encompassing and may be deemed authoritative on doctrine.

For their topic, they also turn out to be unique. That is to say, a quick survey of protracted essays on various topics will yield only one systematic and protracted discussion of any given theme. Thus, on such a subject as honor due to mothers, resurrection of the dead, holiness of the Land, the person of Abraham, circumcision, the Messiah, and the like, we find one substantial aggregate of materials, and the aggregate will be unique in this Talmud. Individual or discrete materials assembled in such constructions may recur many times, to be sure. But as a redactionally whole and complete statement, the encyclopedia article on a stated theme (so far as I can see) does not. Why is this fact important?

It means that the placement, therefore, of such a systematic account of a topic, as much as the *contents*, reveals what the article's organizers deem striking about the topic. In the lengthy discussion of the Messiah (b. San. 99b–102a, cf. *Messiah in Context*), for instance, the issue of the Messiah proved integral to the talmudic redactors' treatment of the Mishnah's chapter on individual Jews' enjoying a portion in the world to come. How so? Mention of the issue of the prevalent thesis of individual teleology—life after death, the world to come—provokes interest in the nation's collective teleology in eschatology. The two dimensions, individual and collective, serve to take the measure of the theme. While, in the end, the discussion of the Messiah in the context of the end of history alongside the individual in the context of death and resurrection yields no systematic account, the point is abundantly clear.

We come now to our topic, the Torah. So far as I am able to tell, we find on the theme of the Torah in the Talmud of Babylonia only one systematic and extensive composition—that is, only one compilation of more than two or three autonomous pericopae. That composition runs on, as we shall now see, for many passages, constituting a lengthy and important statement on its own. The judgment of the framers of the composition on the meaning of the term Torah coincides with the position of the editors of the Talmud on where that discussion should be located. How so? The point of the passage, in recurrent sayings, scriptural exegeses, and tales, is that the most important meaning of the word Torah lies in its defining who is Israel and who is not. The fate of the people Israel rests upon their faith in the Torah, their loyalty to the Torah. And where do the Talmud's redactors choose to place the passage, but in the sole tractate of the Mishnah, hence of the two Talmuds, which addresses the relationship between Israel and the nations of the world?

By placing the composition at the head of Babylonian Talmud tractate Abodah Zarah, which deals with how Israel is to relate to gentiles on those occasions on which the gentile celebrates his pagan cult, the framers of the Talmud endorse the message of the compositors of the compilation. The individual sayings emphasize that Israel is Israel by virtue of the Torah. So the editors sort out Israel's relationships to the gentiles by reference to the Torah. The Deuteronomists would hardly have been surprised: "For that will be your wisdom and your understanding in the sight of the peoples, who, when they hear all these statutes, will say, 'Surely this great nation is a wise and understanding people.' For what great nation is there that has a god so near to it as the Lord our God is to us, whenever we call upon him? And what great nation is there, that has statutes and ordinances so righteous as all this Torah which I set before you this day?" (Deut. 4:6–8). Whether the nations ever agreed (or even knew) is hardly at issue. What is important is the reaffirmation, at the end of the formation of Judaism, of the point at which it had all begun.

We turn now to the construction as a whole, abbreviated so as to omit extraneous material.

B. Abodah Zarah 2b–4a
[Translated by A. Mishcon, pp. 2–11]

I. R. Hanina b. Papa (some say R. Simlai) expounded thus: In times to come, the Holy One, blessed be He, will take a scroll of the Torah in his embrace and proclaim: 'Let him who has occupied himself herewith come and take his reward.' Thereupon all the nations will crowd together in confusion, as it is said, 'All the nations are gathered together' (Is. 43:9). The Holy One . . . will then say to them: 'Come not before Me in confusion, but let each nation come in with its scribes. . . .' Thereupon the Kingdom of Edom [Esau= Rome] will enter first before him. (Why first? Because they are most important. . . .)

The Holy One, blessed be He, will then say to them: 'Wherewith have you occupied yourselves?' They will reply: 'O Lord of the Universe, we have established many market-places, we have erected many baths, we have accumulated much gold and silver, and all this we did only for the sake of Israel, that they might [have leisure] for occupying themselves with the study of the Torah.'

The Holy One, blessed be He, will say in reply: 'You foolish ones among peoples, all that which you have done, you have only done to satisfy your own desires. You have established market-places to place courtesans therein; baths, to revel in them; [as to the distribution of] silver and gold, that is mine, as it is written: *Mine is the silver and Mine is the gold, saith the Lord of Hosts* (Hag. 2:8); are there any among you who have been declaring *this?*' And '*this*' is nought else than the Torah, as it is said: *And* this *is the* Law *which Moses set before the children of Israel* (Deut. 4:44). They will then depart crushed in spirit.

On the departure of the Kingdom of Rome, Persia will step forth. (Why Persia next?—Because they are next in importance.) The Holy One, blessed be He, will ask of them: 'Wherewith have ye occupied yourselves?'; and they will reply 'Sovereign of the Universe, we have built many bridges, we have captured many cities, we have waged many wars, and all this for the sake of Israel, that they might engage in the study of the Torah. Then the Holy One, blessed be He, will say to them: 'You foolish ones among peoples, you have built bridges in order to extract toll, you have subdued cities, so as to impose forced labour; as to waging war, *I* am the Lord of battles, as it is said: *The Lord is a man of war* (Ex. 15:3); are there any amongst you who have been declaring *this?*' and '*this*' means nought else than the Torah, as it is said: *And* this *is the* Law *which Moses set before the children of Israel.* They, too, will then depart crushed in spirit. (But why should the Persians, having seen that the Romans achieved nought, step forward at all?—They will say to themselves: 'The Romans have destroyed the Temple, whereas we have built it.')

And so will every nation fare in turn. (But why should the other nations come forth, seeing that those who preceded them had achieved nought?—They will say to themselves:. The others have oppressed Israel, but we have not. And why are these [two] nations singled out as important, and not the others?—Because their reign will last till the coming of the Messiah.)

The nations will then contend: 'Lord of the Universe, hast Thou given us the Torah, and have we declined to accept it?'

(But how can they argue thus, seeing that it is written, *The Lord came from Sinai and rose from Seir unto them, He shined forth from mount Paran?* (Deut. 33:2). And it is also written, *God cometh from Teman* (Hab. 3:3). What did He seek in Seir, and what did He seek in Mount Paran?—R. Yohanan says: This teaches us that the Holy One, blessed be He, offered the Torah to every nation and every tongue, but none accepted it, until He came to Israel who received it.

[How, then, can they say that the Torah was not offered to them?] Their contention will be this: 'Did we accept it and fail to observe it?' But surely the obvious rejoinder to this their plea would be: 'Then why did you not accept it?'

—This, then, will be their contention: 'Lord of the Universe, didst Thou suspend the mountain over us like a vault as Thou hast done unto Israel and did we still decline to accept it?'

For in commenting on the verse: *And they stood at the nether part of the mountain* (Ex. 19:17), R. Dimi b. Hama said: This teaches us that the Holy One, blessed be He, suspended the mountain over Israel like a vault, and said unto them: 'If ye accept the Torah, it will be well with you, but if not, there will ye find your grave.'

Thereupon the Holy One, blessed be He, will say to them: 'Let us then consider the happenings of old . . . there are seven commandments which you did accept, did you observe them?'

The nations will then say, 'Sovereign of the Universe, has Israel, who accepted the Torah, observed it?' The Holy One, blessed be He, will reply, '*I* can give evidence that they observed the Torah.' 'O Lord of the Universe,' they will argue, 'can a father give evidence in favour of his son? For it is written, *Israel is My son, My firstborn*' (Ex. 4:22). Then will the Holy One, blessed be He, say: 'Heaven and Earth can bear witness that Israel has fulfilled the entire Torah.' But they will [object], saying: 'Lord of the Universe, Heaven and Earth are partial witnesses, for it is said, *If not for My covenant with day and with night, I should not have appointed the ordinances of Heaven and Earth*' (Jer. 33:25).

Then the Holy One, blessed be He, will say, 'Some of yourselves shall testify that Israel observed the entire Torah. Let Nimrod come and testify that Abraham did not [consent to] worship idols; let Laban come and testify that Jacob could not be suspected of theft; let Potiphar's wife testify that Joseph was above suspicion of immorality; let Nebuchadnezzar come and testify that Hanania, Mishael and Azariah did not bow down to an image; let Darius come and testify that Daniel never neglected the [statutory] prayers; let Bildad the Shuhite, and Zophar the Naamathite, and Eliphaz the Temanite [and Elihu the son of Barachel the Buzite] testify that Israel has observed the whole Torah.'

The nations will then plead, 'Offer us the Torah anew and we shall obey it.' But the Holy One, blessed be He, will say to them, 'You foolish ones among peoples, he who took trouble [to prepare] on the eve of the Sabbath can eat on the Sabbath, but he who has not troubled on the eve of the Sabbath, what shall he eat on the Sabbath? Nevertheless, I have an easy command which is called *Sukkah;* go and carry it out.'

Straightaway will every one of them betake himself and go and make a booth on the top of his roof; but the Holy One, blessed be He, will cause the sun to blaze forth over them as at the Summer Solstice, and every one of them will trample down his booth and go away, as it is said, *Let us break their bonds asunder, and cast away their cords from us* (Ps. 2:3).

Thereupon the Holy One, blessed be He, will laugh at them, as it is said, *He that sitteth in heaven laugheth* (Ps. 2:4).

II.   Rab Judah said in the name of Rab: 'The day consists of twelve hours; during the first three hours the Holy One, blessed be He, is occupying Himself with the Torah, during the second three He sits in judgment on the whole world, and when He sees that the world is so guilty as to deserve destruction, He transfers Himself from the seat of Justice to the seat of Mercy; during the third quarter, He is feeding the whole world, from the horned buffalo to the brood of vermin; during the fourth quarter He is sporting with the leviathan. . . . '

III.   R. Levi says: He who discontinues [learning] words of the Torah and indulges in idle gossip will be made to eat glowing coals of juniper, as it is said, *They pluck salt-wort with wormwood; and the roots of juniper are their food* (Job 30:4).

IV.   Resh Lakish says: To him who is engaged in the study of the Torah by night, the Holy One extends a thread of grace by day, as it is said, *By day the Lord will command his lovingkindness, and in the night his song shall be with me* (Ps. 42:9).

V.   Rab Judah says in the name of Samuel: Why is it written, *And Thou makest man as the fishes of the sea, and as the creeping things, that have no ruler over them* (Hab. 1:14)? Why is man here compared to the fishes of the sea? To tell you, just as the fishes of the sea, as soon as they come on to dry land, die, so also man, as soon as he abandons the Torah and the precepts [incurs destruction].

What is important in the present composite is the lengthy opening narrative (I). It speaks neither of the study of Torah, on the one side, nor of the keeping of the teachings of the Torah, on the other. Here the scroll of the Torah—imagined in total abstraction!—serves to distinguish between Israel and the empires, Rome, Persia, then all other nations, and to explain why Israel alone enjoys God's favor. "Torah" is the reason, meaning studying and keeping the Torah, or, in modern language, practicing "Judaism." In the storyteller's vision, the nations seek justification before God by appealing to how they have served the Torah through service to Israel. The humor and irony can scarcely be missed, since God's replies, through the unfolding of the tale, make them explicit. Then the nations exculpate themselves by saying that, after all, God never gave them the Torah anyhow. The story proceeds (in what seems to me a zigzag) to demonstrate that, in any event, Israel did keep the Torah. Gentile witnesses, Laban, Potiphar's wife, Nebuchadnezzar, Darius, and the like, all testify that Israel really did observe the whole Torah. The nations then ask for a chance to keep the Torah and are given it—with disastrous results. The story joins the two principal meanings associated with the Torah, studying it and carrying out its commandments, and in the aggregate makes a fresh and startling point. It is, as I said, that Israel is justified because it has kept and has studied the Torah. This bears obvious implications for what Israel must continue to do. A story such as this shows how the word Torah stands for the doctrine of Judaism.

The remainder of the composite presents no surprises. God spends a fourth of the day studying Torah (II). One who stops learning words of Torah and uses his tongue for gossip will be burned (III). Studying Torah by night, when people usually sleep, is especially meritorious and provokes a good reward (IV). When a person abandons the Torah and commandments, destruction follows (V). All of these are conventional; the purpose in including them, it seems to me, is simply to ring the changes on familiar assertions. They serve to turn the whole into a composite, so the long story becomes something more, as I said at the outset. Now, finally, we have a complete picture of what people call to mind when they speak of the word Torah.

Once the Torah serves to explain the condition of Israel among the nations, we move from the realm of otherworldly discourse about encounter through the Torah with God to the immediate society of flesh-and-blood mortals. For in this last rubric we find how the Torah as an abstract symbol is made to serve the concrete interests of the people Israel, in its this-worldly historical life, its politics, its ongoing social experience. Israel emerged from the formative centuries at hand to live in a single way under diverse circumstances, to shape its life in accordance with the way of Torah. From England in the far north and west to India and even remote China, Jews lived in accordance with the religious system at hand and found it self-evident that the system made sense. So they explained to themselves who they were, and who the nations were, by invoking the message of the Torah much as the story at hand portrayed that message. Judaism, in its final symbolic formulation in the era now closing in the last pages of the Babylonian Talmud, told the people Israel who it was and why it lived where and how it did, who the nations were, and why they treated Israel the way they did (the only thing important, after all, about the nations).

So as uniform symbol of many diverse things, the Torah served to state the substance of the message in every possible medium—material and intellectual, as concrete object, in human form, and as abstract arbiter of matters of status, social and personal. The symbol of the Torah served to classify things on earth and (in the minds of the faithful) in heaven as well. For the succeeding centuries, until nearly our own day, time stood still and life remained the same for Israel under the aspect of the Torah. When we ask for other eternal components of late antiquity's legacy to the West, we find the Torah standing not quite alone, to be sure, but not on a crowded stage: on a dark stage pinpointed in a shaft of light along with philosophy, Christianity, Islam, and law—but not much more.

The important issue confronting any theory of the foundations of Judaism comes at the end: How shall we account for the long centuries of success of Judaism, in the definition it had reached at the end of its formative age in late antiquity, within Israel, the Jewish people? And how shall we account also for the recent success, over the past two hundred years, of competing views within Israel? These two complementary questions frame the critical issue in describing, analyzing and interpreting the history of Judaism in the West. If any effort to explain how it all began is to yield results, the outcome must then encompass two contradictory facts, self-evidence, then oblivion. It is easy enough to account for the first of these. The long-term success of Judaism emerged from these, the formative centuries, when, through the method of exegesis (midrash), the processes of revelation of Torah made provision for the whole of a long future; when, through an eschatology based upon the promise of a Messiah, the results of a long process of defining Torah persuaded the bulk of the people Israel to remain within the system; when, through the conception of Torah as the source of both personal and national salvation, method and teleology and doctrine all fused together. In that long period and over the frontiers of many lands, the people Israel found self-evident the system that explained to Israel, in midrash, Messiah and Torah, whence they had come, whither they must go, and who they now were. Why should the active quest for the Messiah through a passive resignation have succeeded, as it did, in keeping Israel, turbulent nation of old, at peace with itself and its fate as vanquished and subjugated? The obvious answer is that the system fit the facts and thus compelled Israel to accommodate itself to those facts: defeat, abasement, degradation. It turned defeat into victory, abasement into power, degradation into dignity.

For in its stress on an ever-keener mastery of less and less material, on control of those inconsequential matters left in Israel's power by the victorious nations (and, from Israel's viewpoint, Israel was the only loser), the system of sagacious exegesis of Torah, of Messianism carefully calibrated to accord with the quiescent life of Torah, and of salvation attained within the protecting walls of the Torah, did fit the facts. It made the facts appear to accord with, to reinforce, the faith. A system that spoke of salvation in history but effected a life of sanctification beyond time admirably suited the life of a people that endured history, but did not make it. So, we cannot find the outcome astonishing, when, at the climax of the formative centuries, we find claims that the Torah saves Israel, while it also separates Israel from the nations, thus accounting for the condition of Israel in the eyes of the nations.

But why is it, at the other end of time as we now know it, that falling into oblivion, the system lost its self-evidence to the minds of its practitioners? We who have just now witnessed the re-messianization of the system of Judaism in its most classical formulations and expressions—within the pure traditionalism of the Orthodox Judaism of the State of Israel—can only wonder in amazement at this current event in the unpredictable history of the ancient faith of Israel. When Torah-sages discover, through the established processes of Torah-exegesis, that the Messiah is near at hand and will come in response not so much to the life of sanctification led by everyone in their context but more particularly to acts of salvation accomplished by the saving few, in such a setting at least, the old Judaism has come to an end, and a new formation has begun. Why the rabbinic system has changed in its most classical formulation I do not know.

So at the end of the labor of description and analysis of the formation of a longstanding system of Judaism, our frail powers of interpretation fail us, as well they should, when we ask the reason why. God alone knows why. And that is fitting, given the things we study—a religion in its current social context, in its concrete human setting, in its framing in, and shaping of, minds and hearts and hopes.

Index of Passages

BIBLE

OTHER ANCIENT SOURCES

General Index